Vegetable gardening need not be hard work
and it can be enjoyable, so long as you know
how to go about it. In this book, Tom
Wellsted gives invaluable advice on the soil
preparation, sowing and harvesting of herbs and
vegetables that can be grown without the
protection of glass. From artichoke and fennel
to tomato and sweet corn, *Vegetable and
Herb Growing* is an excellent guide for all
lovers of fresh produce who want the
maximum success with the minimum fuss.

Vegetable and Herb Growing

TOM WELLSTED

SPHERE BOOKS LIMITED
30/32 Gray's Inn Road, London WC1X 8JL

First published in Great Britain by Sphere Books Ltd 1977
Copyright © Tom Wellsted 1977
Illustrations copyright © Linden Artists Ltd

Printed in Great Britain by
Hazell Watson & Viney Ltd
Aylesbury, Bucks

Set in Monotype Times

CONTENTS

INTRODUCTION

There are many books on vegetable growing and most of these are very good counsels of perfection. But perfection is costly, whether in time, money or both. And I have no doubt that many with larger gardens than mine will scoff at this book: as one acquaintance has said 'I'm looking forward to being told how to grow vegetables by you.' He has a large garden and can sow to an excess point where failure means he has enough. So why don't I dig up my ornamental plants and do as he does to get enough? Because I have a small garden and I believe a garden is best as a mixture of different plants, mingling as much as possible, and a place to live in with those plants. Who fancies sunbathing lying among the beans or cabbages?

And so, my climbing beans clamber up a net in front of a hedge of holly, hazel, hawthorn and roses and my celeriac is growing well in front of, and partially under, some pink hybrid musk roses. The outdoor cucumbers, tub grown, are now climbing up the buddleias.

The plan of the book is to provide a quick and easy reference for each vegetable that can be grown without the protection of glass. It is therefore not a book for experts and prize growers, but I hope it will help you to grow good vegetables and perhaps suggest that you might grow something you have not tried before.

SOIL

The first thing to tackle is the soil. Here the notes are usually brief and give the type of soil in which it is most suitable to grow the particular vegetable and the situation – most vegetables grow well in a medium loam, previously enriched by well-rotted manure or compost, and in a sunny site. The latter is usually easier than the former, especially in new gardens where the soil might be in poor condition. So what is the meaning of a good medium loam? A good loam has the necessary consistency for plant growth, with enough of the necessary minerals and other elements for that growth, and which, while being moisture retentive, is well-drained and will not drown the plant roots by excluding air. All soils can be improved, whether they are heavy or light, by regularly digging in well-rotted manure or compost.

Manure can be difficult to get but compost is a natural by-product of good gardening. And as our local council pointed out a few years ago, the compost can be enriched by using household slops – the contents of chamber pots – diluted one part urine to twenty parts water which is poured on the compost heap. Virtually anything which will rot down may be used but it is wiser not to put too much slow-rotting material – wood for instance – into a heap. There are several 'compost makers' on the market, most rather like perforated dustbins and all quite expensive. Wooden planks or chicken wire with suitable corner posts can both be used to make a container. Polythene, preferably black, can be used to cap the heap inside the container to help to get up heat. Turn the mixture – inside out – every so often to ensure an evenly rotted mixture. When the compost is ready it will be of a friable composition, rather like soil, and rich brown in colour. On heavy soils, sharp sand can be added with benefit. Sharp sand is so called because the edges of the grains have not been rounded off by water, or other action, and therefore provides a better drainage material, keeping the soil open. Peat is expensive but when other forms of humus (manure, compost) are not available, it can be added as a start until your own compost heap is producing. Peat is usually sterile and does not contain plant foods so these have to be added. A good additive is fish manure as its organic content stimulates worm activity and worms improve the soil by increasing the drainage, and contributing a certain amount of humus.

Poor heavy soils, will be improved by digging which allows the winter frosts to break down the large clumps, and by adding whatever compost, manure or peat is available. Lime should be used with caution and according to the nature of the soil you have – local opinions can be a help here but you can also establish more positively the balance of your soil by testing it with one of the small soil testing kits on sale. Some weeks before planting is to commence, rake the soil down to a finer tilth – as fine as you can for seed beds. At this stage a general fertiliser can be sprinkled and raked in to help give your plants a good start. Prior to sowing and planting in a bed that has recently been converted from lawn, it can be a good thing to dust it with a pesticide, such as BHC powder, to help control leatherjackets. These eat plant roots and often cause what appears to be the sudden and mysterious collapse of a seedling.

SOWING AND PLANTING

Though you can get away with a surprising amount of not doing what you should, it does pay in the successful raising of seeds to sow in a well-dug and de-stoned soil. So, after digging, even if you have not the time to rake the whole bed down, do rake the rows as free from stones as you can. Sowing is then a simple matter; take a hoe, or stick, and draw out a line at the appropriate depth or prod a suitable hole. Then sow; fine seeds generally as thinly as you can, larger seeds such as beetroot and spinach can be individually placed. Cover the seeds and water with a spray. The watering settles the seeds in, as well as softening the seed skin, and so makes for easier germination. Reasonably fine soil, which can be easily dug out and replaced, greatly facilitates planting by allowing the soil to be more easily mingled with the roots as it is replaced. Again, water plants in to help settle the soil around the roots.

CULTIVATION

Cultivation is largely a matter of common sense. In drying weather all plants will need more water to be provided. Drying weather is especially damaging to newly planted out plants and will probably occur more frequently through the action of the wind rather than the sun. Spraying over plants, so that the leaves can quickly absorb the moisture, is also beneficial though it does not preclude a good soaking of the ground. Superficial watering tends to bring the roots to the surface, making the plants still more vulnerable to drying weather. Weeding need not be total but should be done bearing in mind that weeds rob the soil of plant nutrients and water, may keep the soil cooler than desired, may harbour pests and help thereby in the distribution of disease and provide seeds for a future, unwanted, crop. Keep weeds down, therefore, near the plants and prevent those further away from seeding and growing where you are keeping weeds under control. In a small garden, hand weeding is unbeatable in efficiency and cost. Hoeing is fine if you have the time to do it again and again and yet again; but it can also provide the right conditions for propagating more weeds. Most of the weedkillers available are more suited to commercial enterprises except for preparation of the ground before sowing or planting. Some persist in the soil for a time and care should be taken in selecting one. Paraquat, marketed as Weedol, breaks down and is probably the most useful in the small garden. It is fairly expensive but can save time if the right weather conditions, reasonable sun and little wind, prevail. Pests are more complex to deal with, but can be treated with reasonable efficiency bearing in mind that they fall into three main types: soil-borne minute pests such as eelworms – of these, the main ones are mentioned and their control indicated under the appropriate vegetable; soil-borne larger pests such as leatherjackets which can be controlled by dusting sowing rows or planting sites with BHC dust (leatherjackets should never be forgotten if you are using a new bed dug from recent lawn); and lastly, air-borne pests such as greenfly, which I now control by not spraying for this may also kill off their natural predators such as ladybirds, lacewings and their respective larvae. Unless you have a very large garden and you are reasonably vigilant caterpillars can best be dealt with by hand picking. Slugs may be controlled by using a proprietary slug-killer. I have found the bran-type Slug Death the best and it is also comparatively inexpensive. Rotation of crops and regular digging to keep the soil in good condition, with the addition of compost, is one of the best controls for general soil-borne pests and diseases, making devastation of epidemic proportions unlikely.

HARVESTING

Timing your harvesting is usually obvious, but the less obvious, such as sweet corn, are mentioned later under their specific vegetable headings.

VARIETIES

New varieties of most vegetables are being continually produced. F_1 hybrids are available for a number of vegetables now and are usually more vigorous than ordinary sorts. They will not come true from seed saved from them. Some are improvements, while others may not be. Some 'new' vegetables, much lauded by their seedsmen, are both time and money wasting. On the other hand, two modern varieties to my palate and patience are outstanding improvements. These are the white beetroot, which provides an excellent root as well as edible stalks and leaves, and the Burpless cucumbers which are of very good flavour and texture, superior to most greenhouse varieties, and of easy cultivation. The white beetroot can be obtained from Messrs Thompson and Morgan, Ipswich, Suffolk, while the Burpless cucumbers are now widely available. There are large numbers of small, reputable seed firms, though they may tend to cater for specialists. Their names and addresses and the specialities they cater for may be found in the horticultural magazines and papers. Most seeds can be obtained from one of the larger, nationally known establishments, listed below. Postal charges, especially for heavy seeds such as peas and beans, may be high but can often be avoided by buying from some of the stores which make a feature of garden requirements, such as Woolworths, as well, of course, from one of the independent garden shops. These can be useful if they stock a good selection of seeds from different seedsmen so that most requirements can be supplied. Varietal names are being standardised now so that seedsman 'A' will have to offer the same plant as seedsman 'B' under the same name, for at present many so-called varieties are merely the same plants under another name. This standardisation is one benefit which joining the European Economic Community has brought about, and it is to be applauded.

Varieties especially recommended for flavour are marked †, and those suitable for freezing are marked *.

S E Marshall & Co Ltd, Oldfield Lane, Wisbech, Cambs.
Samuel Dobie & Son Ltd, Upper Dee Mills, Llangollen, Clwyd LL20 8SD
Suttons Seeds Ltd, London Road, Earley, Reading, Berkshire RG6 1AB
Thompson & Morgan (Ipswich) Ltd, London Road, Ipswich, Suffolk IP2 0BA

ARTICHOKE, GLOBE

GENERAL

Very ornamental plants to grow if you have the space for them. In small gardens a few can be grown as part of the herbaceous border, in a carefully chosen position, for they have a spread of several feet and may grow up to 6 feet in height. Besides the 'globe', the side shoots, known as chards can be eaten raw like celery but it is better to let the strength go into the plant for the next year.

SOIL

Well-drained but with plenty or manure or compost added. Choose a sunny site.

SOW OR PLANT

They may be grown from seed sown outdoors from mid-March in the south, from May in the north, and up to the late summer. Early sowings should provide 'globes' the same year. Suckers may be planted in April and a sprinkle of general fertiliser added then.

CULTIVATION

Little attention is needed once they are growing, but keep watered and feed occasionally. Plants should last for 5 to 6 years but most people renew after 3 years for the better quality of young plants. For good quality restrict each plant to a maximum of 3 heads. It is best to protect them during the winter with a covering of straw or other handy material or the plants may be killed by frost. Usually untroubled by pests or diseases, though blackfly may be unsightly, and young plants and chards are tasty to slugs – a commercial slug killer should be used.

To blanch the artichoke shoots, tie the leaf bunch together when a couple of feet long, and cover with black polythene.

CROP

Globes from late June, chards from late autumn.

VARIETIES

Green Ball.
Gros vert de Laon.

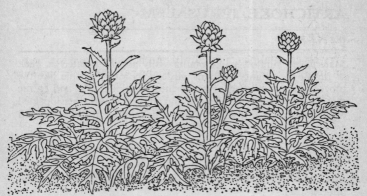

Young plants in bud

Heeling in suckers, 2–3 feet apart

Cut before the bud opens – not as below

Blanching

ARTICHOKE, JERUSALEM

GENERAL

Magnificent sunflower-like plants easily accommodated as back of the border plants in small gardens. A lot of people like the tuberous roots cooked or made into soup. I don't, and to me this is a salad vegetable, cleaned and cut into dice (rather lopsided ones) and eaten raw – they have a delicious nutty flavour and crispness. Easy growing plants.

SOIL

Any, with reasonable drainage, in a fairly sunny site. Manure not required.

PLANT

Tubers should be planted where they are to grow in February or March.

CULTIVATION

Little attention is required; they grow like sunflowers 5 to 7 feet high and so may require staking or stringing up to prevent untidiness, however, if you do not want the flowers then cut the stems to 4 to 5 feet and save staking. They do not require feeding. They can spread quite a bit and to prevent this make sure that all the tubers are dug up when harvesting – the smaller ones can then be stored to provide next year's plants. Unlikely to be troubled by pests or diseases.

CROP

Late autumn, and through the winter

RECOMMENDED VARIETIES

Fuseau, smoother skinned than most.

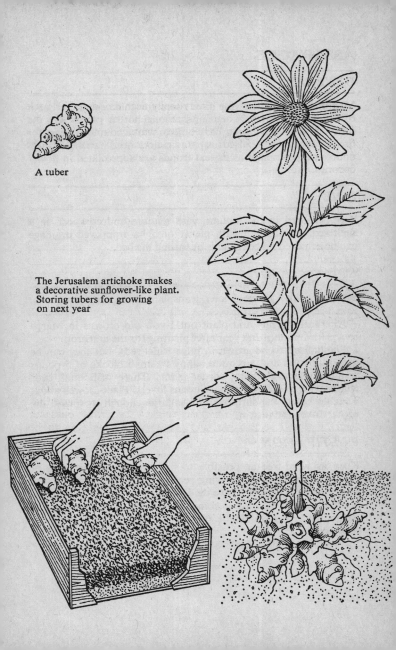

A tuber

The Jerusalem artichoke makes
a decorative sunflower-like plant.
Storing tubers for growing
on next year

ASPARAGUS

GENERAL

You might not think you have room for this vegetable, but it can be grown in small beds and among border plants. On the other hand you might not have time to wait a couple of years for its potential to be realised: asparagus does need patience. It is a double-purpose plant as its leaf fronds are appreciated in flower decorations.

SOIL

Well-prepared in the autumn with manure and compost, in a sheltered position but with plenty of light. Improved drainage can be achieved on heavy soils by raising the bed.

SOW OR PLANT

Sow seeds in April and later transplant into permanent beds: wait 3 years for first crop.

Alternatively buy and plant out 1-year-old crowns in March to April: wait until 2nd year after planting for the first crop.

Plants used to be grown in huge wide beds, but they can be grown in rows and are quite happy in small blocks of 5 plants in a yard square among border plants. Three such small beds will provide ample for two asparagus lovers. Plant crowns about 4 inches below the surface in holes large enough to spread the roots. Cover and firm in.

CULTIVATION

Keep as weed-free as possible to prevent unnecessary loss of water. Keep moist in growing season. In the autumn cut the plants down, when they have died back, to an inch or so; mulch, preferably with manure or compost. Main bug is the asparagus beetle: its grubs should be destroyed with an appropriate insecticide.

CROP

When the crowns have become established (see Sow or Plant above) don't cut everything that grows for the first crop in May – just take from each plant a couple of shoots about 9 inches long, that is when they are 4 to 5 inches above ground. As plants become established more shoots will develop and the season can be extended into June.

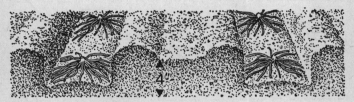

Spread the roots when planting

A small asparagus bed, 1 yard square, for the border

RECOMMENDED VARIETIES

Brocks Imperial F$_1$ – a new variety available as seed.
Connovers Colossal – old established variety, widely available.
Martha Washington – from America available as seed.
Regal, Paske's Regal Pedigree – very succulent.

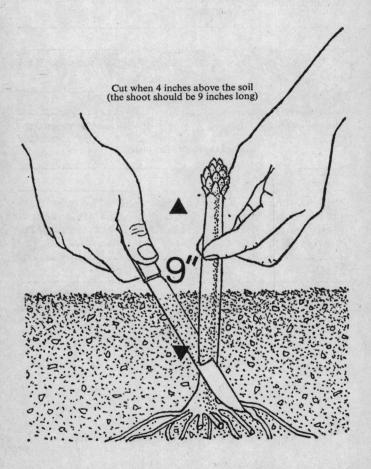

Cut when 4 inches above the soil
(the shoot should be 9 inches long)

9"

BASIL

GENERAL

I can do no better than begin by quoting from Tom Stobart in his *Herbs, Spices and Flavourings*, '. . . basil is one of the great culinary herbs . . .'. An easily grown annual reaching 1 to 3 feet in height. The leaves can be used to flavour most meats, fish as well as egg dishes, soups and in salads.

SOIL

Well-drained soil in a warm and sunny spot, sheltered from winds.

SOW

As basil ages it toughens and tends to lose its flavour so successional sowings providing a regular supply of young plants are best. Sow in March into seed trays.

CULTIVATION

Prick out when large enough to handle and plant into pots. Plant out, after hardening off the seedlings. If you are not eating it quickly enough, you can pinch out shoots to make it bushy. Believe it or not, it is hardly troubled by pests and diseases.

CROP

As required, from May until the plants are killed by the weather (or run out, of course). Use whole leaves in cooking as they give a better flavour.

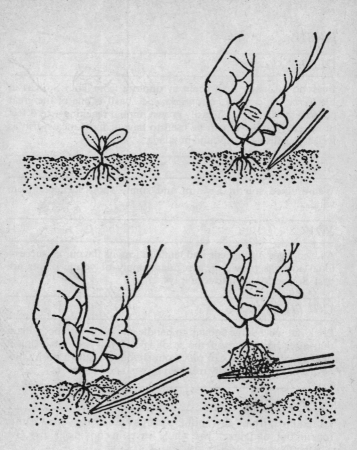

Prick out seedlings when large enough
to handle, taking care not to damage the
young roots

Prick out the young tip to make bushy

Growing on a window sill

BAY

GENERAL

An essential culinary plant and ornamental too. It will, if allowed, make quite a large tree, but is usually grown as a bush. Amenable to clipping to the extent of topiary work. Will grow up to 15 feet or more unless restricted by clipping.

SOIL

Any good garden soil but in a sheltered sunny position for preference. If grown in a tub, use prepared soils such as John Innes or Levington.

PLANT

Plant in spring and as for any shrub, ensure the ground has been dug. Firm the plant in by tramping around it, provided the ground is in suitable condition. If you are planting a large specimen make sure it is adequately staked and preferably put the stake in before the plant.

CULTIVATION

Keep reasonably moist until established. Scale insects are the chief pest and they exude a sticky substance. Apart from this nuisance value it is hardly worth treating well-established bushes.

CROP

Leaves can be picked throughout the year, and used either fresh or dried.

RECOMMENDED VARIETIES

Laurus nobilis, the Sweet Bay or Bay Laurel, is the only species generally cultivated in Britain but there is also a narrow-leaved form, the Willow-leaf Bay, *Laurus nobilis angustifolia*.

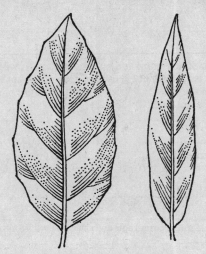

Common bay and Willow-leaf bay

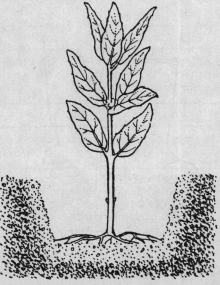

When planting make sure hole is wide enough as well as deep enough

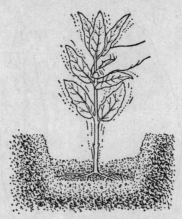

Sprinkle soil to cover roots and shake the soil between them

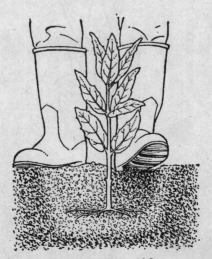

Fill planting hole and firm

BEAN, BROAD

GENERAL

There are two main types of broad bean – Windsor and Longpod. Windsors have short, broad pods containing flatter and broader beans than the Longpods which have longer and rounder pods containing rounder beans. Then there is the early cropping type exemplified by Aquadulce Claudia, which can be sown from October or November in the south and from January in the north. This means that the ground can be cleared for a new crop of some later vegetable: valuable for those with small gardens. Within these groups there are green and white seeded types but the colour has little bearing on flavour.

SOIL

A good medium loam: add plenty of humus to light and heavy soils and manure all. Fishmeal at 3 oz a square yard added before sowing main crops, or in early spring for the early crops, is beneficial. Acid soil should have a little lime scattered.

SOW

Broad beans are usually sown in double rows; this is not essential but pays off in small gardens. October to January for early; February to April for main crops.

CULTIVATION

Except for dwarf varieties support – net or wrap-around strings – is essential. Pinch out the top tip when plants are flowering and setting pods: this discourages blackfly and helps fill the pods. Usually no trouble is caused by diseases or pests except for black-fly.

CROP

When seeds are $\frac{1}{2}$ to $\frac{3}{4}$ inches across. This will be from May for the earlies in a good season, to July.

Beans sown in a double row before
covering. Beans should be 3 inches
deep and 6 inches apart

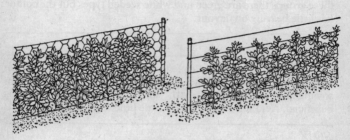

Methods of support

Pinch out the growing tip

RECOMMENDED VARIETIES (*all* *)

Aquadulce (Giant Seville) – 8 beans, early.
Aquadulce Claudia (Mammoth Seville) – 8–9 beans, early.
Imperial Green Longpod – 9 beans, main crop.
Imperial Green Windsor – 7 beans, main crop.
Imperial White Longpod – 9–10 beans, main crop.
Imperial White Windsor – 8 beans, main crop.
The Sutton – dwarf, 4–5 beans, main crop.

BEAN, CLIMBING

GENERAL

To most people in Britain the runner bean is the only climbing bean. On the Continent almost the complete opposite obtains and a climbing bean means a pole or climbing French bean. The climbing French beans produce pods similar in shape, colour and flavour to dwarf French beans but where bed space is short take up comparatively little room. For elderly people there is an advantage in that cropping does not take place at ground level as with the dwarf bean. Which type to grow is a matter of preference – some people consider the flavour of one to be better than the other. If runner beans are picked young and cooked whole, or snapped in two to fit into the saucepan, they may be very tasty. If for any reason your runners run away, say through your absence on holiday, the mature shelled beans may be used like broad beans and make a very appetising dish. An important gardening difference is that the runner does not produce its seed leaves (cotyledons) above ground level as does the French bean. Therefore well-manured, firm ground and firmed in seeds are required for runners; well manured, but not hard firmed ground – just lightly covered and tramped down – is required for climbing French.

SOIL

Dig as deep as you can and add as much manure as possible. Strawy material is of benefit for it provides, as it rots, a suitable structure in the firmed soil for runner beans to root in.

Sowing beans: 3 inches deep, 6 inches apart for climbing French, 9 inches apart for runner

SOW

Under glass from April to May – cold frame or cold greenhouse to plant out in June; or under cloches in growing position: the cloches should be placed over the ground some weeks before to help warm it up. In the open from May. Sow extra seeds to replace those that fail. Supports should reach about 8 feet high – bamboo stakes should be tied a few inches down from the top to form a cross. On top of the crosses in the row tie in horizontal bamboo stakes for extra strength. With net supports a wire or strong, tight nylon string, stretched between strong supporting posts should suffice.

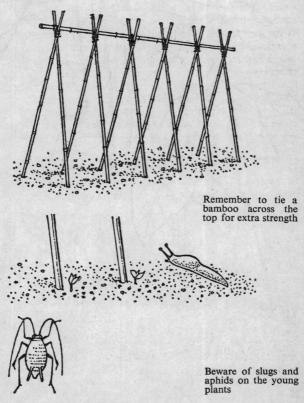

Remember to tie a bamboo across the top for extra strength

Beware of slugs and aphids on the young plants

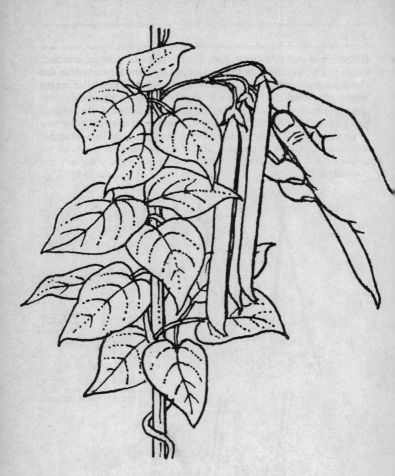

Crop before beans get large and tough

CULTIVATION

Keep as weed-free as possible and make sure the ground is moist; spray the plants when in flower to help set the beans. Aphids are the most noticeable pest on growing plants but at earlier stages slugs, millipedes and grubs of the bean seed fly may take their toll. Diseases may occur but are not often of great importance to the amateur. The variety Kelvedon Marvel may be grown as a 'ground bean' without support – the tops pinched out – and it will then crop a week or two earlier.

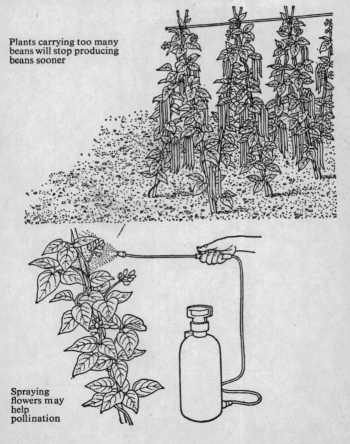

Plants carrying too many beans will stop producing beans sooner

Spraying flowers may help pollination

CROP

Regularly – the more often, the more will be produced in good seasons.

RECOMMENDED VARIETIES

Runner beans: Achievement.*†
     Enorma.*
     Kelvedon Marvel (early).
Climbing French: Romano.*
      Purple podded.*†
      Blue Lake.*

BEAN, DWARF FRENCH

GENERAL

Excellently flavoured vegetables, easy cropping in warm summers
and which, after bearing, should be left in the soil; then top them
and dig the roots in. The roots 'fix' nitrogen which then becomes
available for the next year's crop.

SOIL

Preferably good, but will tolerate a wide range if soil is warm and
moist. Even better if humus in compost or manure form is dug
in during the autumn.

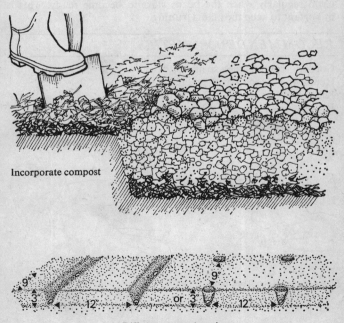

Incorporate compost

Different ways of sowing

SOW

Sow under cloches in March to April or in the open April to May. Early dates for south and good seasons, late for north, cold areas and poor seasons. Do not firm in the beans but cover and press lightly. Water.

CULTIVATION

Keep weed-free: the plants are not deep rooted so weeds will rob them of food and moisture. Main pest is blackfly which may smother plants, reduce and distort crop. Disease unlikely to trouble; destroy if it does.

CROP

Crop regularly when the beans start to become ready. This is important to keep the plants fruiting.

RECOMMENDED VARIETIES

Cordon – round, green stringless.*
Deuil Fin Precoce – oval, green.†
Kinghorn Wax – oval, yellow stringless.*
Royalty – oval, purple stringless.*†

Keep weed-free

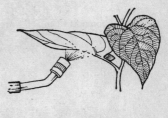

Spray under as well as above leaves to keep aphids under control

34

BEETROOT

GENERAL

Until recently few people thought of beetroot as being more than globe or long-rooted and always of a crimson colour. The crimson globe and long-rooted still exist but we now also have white and yellow globe-rooted varieties. These have advantages: their leaves are excellent used as spinach and they do not 'bleed' like the crimson varieties, but their flavour is sweeter. I have found the white quicker growing and of better flavour than the yellow. Globe varieties are less likely to bolt than the long-rooted varieties.

SOIL

Preferably medium light; heavy soils should have plenty of compost, peat or well-rotted manure added. All soils should be fertile and well-cultivated in early winter. Add 2 oz of a general fertiliser per square yard before sowing. Tomato fertilisers are excellent being rich in potash which beetroot appreciates.

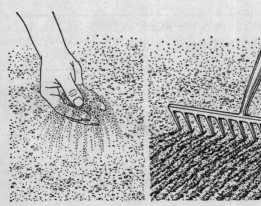

Sprinkle fertiliser evenly   Rake to a fine tilth

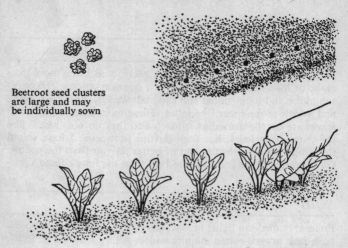

Beetroot seed clusters
are large and may
be individually sown

Thin out to 6 inches apart

SOW

Sow successively from late March to late July in the south; from early April to early July in the north. Sow thinly. Cover. Water.

CULTIVATION

Keep weed-free. Pests not usually troublesome. Diseases may occur but are rarely epidemic.

CROP

As soon as ready when tender. The white and yellow varieties may have leaves pulled but if you want a good 'spinach' crop, leave until a fine head has developed. Protect overwinter crops with straw or lift and store in deep boxes of peat or sand in frost-proof shed. Stored beetroot should have the tops cut off a few inches above the root.

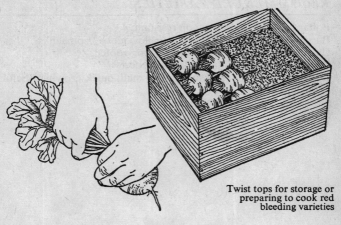

Twist tops for storage or
preparing to cook red
bleeding varieties

A fine head of globe beetroot may
be used as spinach

RECOMMENDED VARIETIES

Boltardy – crimson globe, bolt resistant.
Burpees Golden (Golden Beet) – yellow globe, 'spinach'.†
Cheltenham Green Top – crimson, long-rooted.
Detroit (Crimson Globe) – old favourite.†
Detroit Little Ball – crimson globe, small, quick growing, useful for late sowings.*
Snowhite – white globe, 'spinach'.†

BROCCOLI, SPROUTING

GENERAL

Sprouting broccoli has sprays of whitish, green or purplish heads which appear from the leaf axils through winter and spring, depending on variety. Winter broccoli has a large head (known as a curd) like a cauliflower and is dealt with under that heading. All are developed from the wild cabbage. Excellent small garden vegetables with a long picking season, sometimes picked too late, often overcooked. Nine Star Perennial grows for several years and produces a late spring crop.

SOIL

In a sunny well-drained position, dig in manure or compost in winter. If the soil is not limy, add carbonate of lime in spring at about 4 oz to the square yard. Alternatively, if the soil is in good condition from an earlier crop, lightly fork over and scatter a general fertiliser at about 2 oz to the square yard and hoe it in before planting out.

SOW

In a seed bed April to May. The green Calabrese or Italian sprouting may be sown in early spring under glass for an earlier crop.

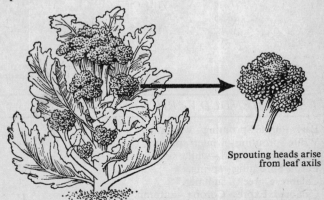

Sprouting heads arise
from leaf axils

CULTIVATION

Plant out in June to July. Keep as weed-free as reasonable. Pests and diseases are those typical of the cabbage family and should be treated similarly. See Cabbage and Savoy.

CROP

According to variety from late summer to spring. After the first cut, a second crop may grow.

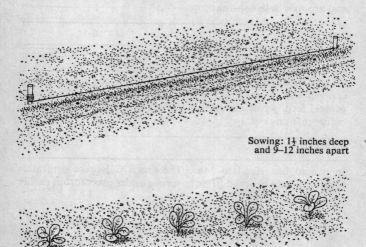

Sowing: 1½ inches deep
and 9–12 inches apart

A thinned-out row: plants
18–24 inches apart

RECOMMENDED VARIETIES

Early Purple Sprouting – winter.*
White Sprouting – winter–spring.
Nine Star Perennial – white, spring.
Purple Sprouting – spring.
Calabrese, green – summer.*
Calabrese Express Corona – autumn.*

BRUSSELS SPROUT

GENERAL

An excellent autumn and winter vegetable. Varieties are now available for successional cropping from about August to April – depending both on variety and the weather. There is also a red sprout available. Sprouts are usually abused in the kitchen – they only need a few minutes in boiling water.

SOIL

Dig in manure or compost in the autumn; scatter a complete fertiliser in the spring at about 3 oz to the square yard.

SOW

If you have any glass, early crops can be produced by sowing during January and February. Main crops should be sown during March and April.

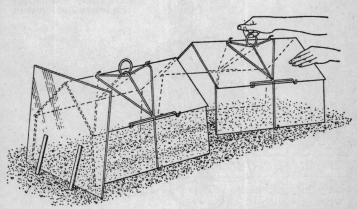

Cloches may be used to
raise early plants

CULTIVATION

Plant out in firm soil when there are four or six leaves and keep them moist until they are re-established. Maturing can be speeded up by 'stopping' the plants – removing the terminal shoot – about October and before the sprouts are firm. Sprouts are a cabbage variety, prone to all the cabbage pests and diseases, and thus require similar treatments. See Cabbage and Savoy.

CROP

Gather as the sprouts ripen, September to February, from the bottom of the stem upwards. When the sprouts are finished the tops can be cooked and eaten.

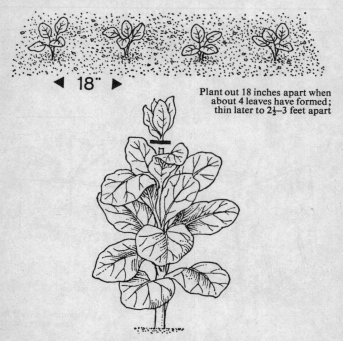

◄ 18" ►

Plant out 18 inches apart when about 4 leaves have formed; thin later to 2½–3 feet apart

Stop by pinching out growing tips to speed maturity

RECOMMENDED VARIETIES

Peer Gynt – compact, early, October to December.*
Citadel – later, December onwards.*
Rubine (Red) – red sprouts, interesting flavour.

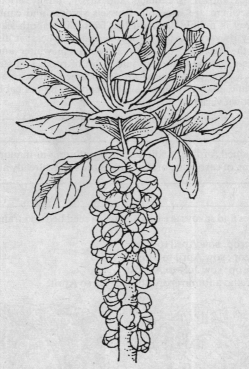

A good crop of sprouts; the tops provide 'greens'

CABBAGE AND SAVOY

GENERAL

The wild cabbage has given rise to a large number of cultivated varieties, mainly for the vegetable garden, though there are some grown for their ornamental value. Here I am dealing with the vegetables known as cabbage and savoy; other varieties dealt with elsewhere are broccoli, Brussels sprouts and cauliflowers. The savoy is mainly distinguished from the smooth-leaved cabbages by its very corrugated leaves and crispness: it also fills a gap in the cabbage succession between the winter and spring croppers. Cabbages take up quite a bit of room and stay in the soil for a long time: therefore only choice varieties are really worthwhile unless you have a lot of room. The red cabbage is a spring-sown variety.

SOIL

Well-drained, ordinary soil prepared with dug-in manure, and a sprinkling of carbonate of lime unless the soil is already alkaline.

SOW

Cabbages and savoys are best sown in a seed bed and transplanted later.
Winter crop: sow April to June.
Savoy crop: sow April to May.
Spring crop: sow July to August.
Summer and autumn crop: sow March to April.

Typical cabbage and savoy

CULTIVATION

Cabbage root fly and caterpillars are the main pests, and club-root the main disease. Suitable chemicals should be applied: trichlorophon for the pests, drenching the soil for the root fly grubs which are root eaters, and the leaves for the caterpillars; club-root, prevalent in badly-drained acid soils, can be controlled to a certain extent by sprinkling hydrated lime and adding a sprinkle of calomel when planting. Don't let beds get too weedy, especially near the plants.

Winter crop: plant out May to July.

Savoy crop: plant out July and August.

Spring crop: plant out September and October.

Summer and autumn crop: plant out June and July.

Sow in drills ½–¾ inch deep, 18 inches apart

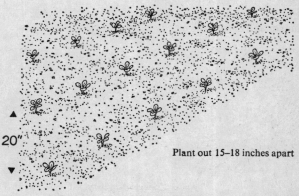

Plant out 15–18 inches apart

CROP

Most of the year, according to the varieties and season.

RECOMMENDED VARIETIES

Winter crop: Christmas Drumhead.

Savoy: Ormskirk, Ostara.

Spring crop: Wheelers Imperial, Offenham – Flower of Spring for spring greens.

Summer and autumn crop: Golden Acre, Niggerhead (Blood Red).

Club root

CARROT

GENERAL

Round, intermediate or long-rooted varieties are available. The round and shorter intermediates are useful on shallow or heavy, stony soils, while the long-rooted varieties fare better on the lighter soils.

SOIL

As with most root crops, carrots do best in a light soil, as stone-free as possible. The soil should have been manured for a previous crop. On heavy and stony soils it can be extremely difficult to grow carrots. In fact I know several keen gardeners in my part of Buckinghamshire who have abandoned these vegetables because of their stony ground, but I have found the round ones do reasonably well. Do not use fresh manure – it leads to root forking.

SOW

From early March to early July: the number of successional sowings depends on the space, and the more space the sooner the next sowing – 2 weeks apart if you have the space, 3 or even 4 weeks in smaller gardens.

CULTIVATION

Thin out regularly. Carrot fly can be a great nuisance but can be avoided by using a seed dressing formulated for this purpose, or by dusting the rows with a suitable insecticide as you sow.

CROP

June and July onwards. Store full-sized carrots by lifting from mid-October, retaining only undamaged roots. Cut leaves about $\frac{1}{2}$ inch from the root top and place carrots in layers, with sand between, in boxes kept in a frost-free, dry shed or other similar place.

Early French Frame (Paris Forcing) – round.
Amsterdam Forcing Amstel – short.*
Chantenay Red Cored – stump.*
St Valery – long.

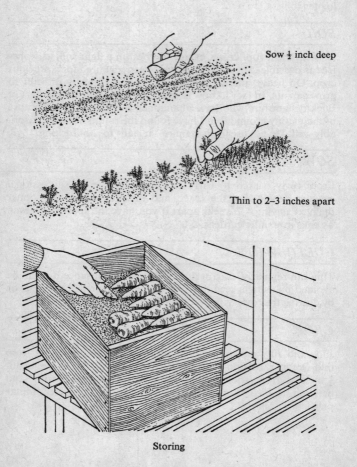

Sow ½ inch deep

Thin to 2–3 inches apart

Storing

CAULIFLOWER AND WINTER BROCCOLI

GENERAL

For all intents and purposes, cauliflower and winter broccoli are the same, for they are varieties of the same plant. Cauliflowers, according to variety and weather, are harvestable from May to December. The winter broccoli fills the gap, maturing between November and June. The two most important points in growing cauliflowers are first, the ground simply must be well-manured, and second, the plants should have no check in growing – such as getting too dry in fine weather. Class 4 below produces heads (known as curds) of excellent quality but they are smaller in size than Class 3 and may therefore be planted closer together.

SOIL

As previously mentioned, it must be well-manured and fertile and the bed should be in a sunny position. Add carbonate of lime to all soils except those already limy – about 4 oz to the square yard.

SOW

There are four classes of cauliflower and winter broccoli makes a fifth. The numbers given subsequently refer to these five groups.
1 Early: sown in September in frames or indoors using a seedbox on a window sill in January.
2 Later maturing than (1) but sown at the same time or may be sown outside in April for a later crop.
3 Sown outside from March to May in rows.
4 Australian varieties sown outside April to May.
5 Winter broccoli is sown as for (3) but English Winter types should not be sown before May from the midlands north; the others are not suitable for growing in cold areas but are excellent in the south.

CULTIVATION

A couple of weeks before planting, add a general fertilizer at the recommended rate given on the bag. Prick out seedlings of (1) and (2), and grow them on, at about $2\frac{1}{2}$ inches apart, in boxes. Harden them off in March and transplant in April. Make sure that the soil is kept moist at all times, especially when pricking out and transplanting as a check will help produce poor curds. Classes (3), (4) and (5) should be thinned out as necessary to prevent overcrowding and loss of vigour. Transplant when they are large enough, which will vary according to when they have been sown, as with (1) and (2). As for (1) and (2), make sure that no check in growth is allowed. Alternatively, they may be thinned further, leaving the strongest growing plants to grow on – 18 inches apart provides, for (4) and (5), only a guide and a few inches either way will make little difference; similarly for (3): 24 inches is a guide. See the pests and diseases comments under Cabbage.

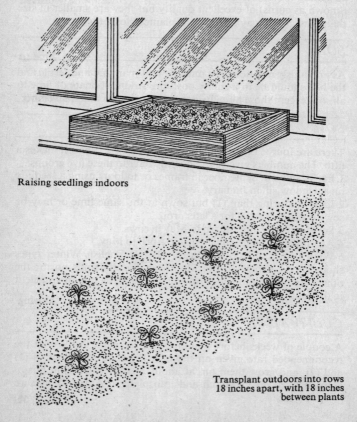

Raising seedlings indoors

Transplant outdoors into rows
18 inches apart, with 18 inches
between plants

CROP

1 Late May to June.
2 June to July or August if April sown.
3 and 4 September to December.
5 November to June, according to variety.

RECOMMENDED VARIETIES

There are a large number of varieties available and new ones are being added to the lists year by year. Catalogues should therefore be used as a guide for advances but those given below have proved their worth:

1 Snowball – June*
  Dominant – July*

2 All the Year Round – crops according to when sown, June to July or August*

3 Flora Blanca Algromajo No. 2 – September to October*
  Autumn Giant Veitch's Self-protecting – October to November
  Autumn Giant Veitch's – November to December

4 Barrier Reef – October
  Canberra – October to November*
  Snowcap – November to December*

5 All the varieties shown below are suitable for growing in the southern counties.

Not for growing in the south west or midlands north.
  Anger's No. 1 – December to February
  Anger's No. 2 – February to March

Not for sowing midlands north before May
  Walcheren Winter varieties – April to May
  English Winter St George – March to April
  English Winter Late Queen – May
  English Winter June Market – May to June

Roscoff varieties should be grown in the south west, maturing according to variety, November to May.

Fold over leaves to keep curd white

CELERY AND CELERIAC

GENERAL

Celeriac is a celery with a large round root and a tuft of celery leaves on top: the root tastes the same as celery root and 'heart' but the celeriac root has to be cut up to be eaten. As I like celery root and heart the best, celeriac is a natural for me. Now celery varieties have been so improved that many of the early bugbears associated with raising it – the expense of labour and cash in glass and so on – may be avoided. Why spend ages blanching by earthing up or putting collars around them, when varieties are available which don't need it, and as they don't need it, celery becomes a plant quite suitable for the small garden.

SOIL

Rich, well-drained and in a sunny position. Dig deeply – 18 inches if you insist on the blanched varieties.

SOW

March to April in seedboxes or pans indoors for blanching, April for self-blanching. Seed is usually treated to prevent disease and it is advisable to wash after handling it.

CULTIVATION

When the seedlings are large enough to handle, prick out into boxes of potting compost. Plant out in June. Self-blanching celery, and also celeriac, may be grown in rows much closer together, about 9 to 12 inches apart, than the trenched, blanching types, which is grown about 3 feet apart. Self-blanching celery may also be grown in squares with about 9 inches between plants. You can use the space on either side of the non self-blanching celery plants for quick crops of lettuce or radishes before it is used to earth up the celery. This is started when the plants are a foot or so high and proceeds in three stages: first as mentioned at about 1 foot; then 3 weeks later to below the lea___ ___ ___ after a further 3 weeks. Before starting the eart___ stems loosely together to prevent soil falling bet___ and wrap in newspaper or black polythene. Keep all times with plenty of water. Carrot fly can be a nuisance, damaging the roots, while celery fly attacks the leaves; slugs complete the job by eating every part of the plant, especially the blanching types after earthing up. There are various proprietary chemicals to deal with these pests – but for carrot fly you must be prepared to apply the chemical to the soil and seed when sowing.

CROP

Celery and celeriac are both late croppers, from the autumn into winter.

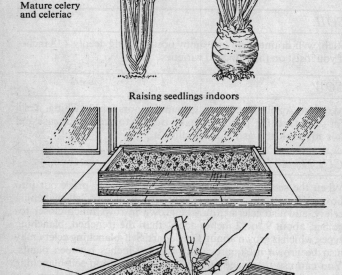

Mature celery
and celeriac

Raising seedlings indoors

Prick out when large enough to handle, 2 inches × 2 inches

Set celery to be blanched 3 feet apart

Tie round some paper to keep the stems
clean and earth up gradually

RECOMMENDED VARIETIES

Self-blanching celery: American Green
                               Golden Self-blanching – dwarf, early.
Trenching celery: Giant White
                            Giant Pink.
Celeriac: Globus
             Invictus.

CHICORY

GENERAL

Chicory has unfortunately suffered some confusion of name with endive: both are different species of the same genus. The name chicory here refers to *Chichorium intybus* and forms. *Chichorium endivia* is described under Endive. The confusion is international: North Americans call the chicory described here endive; but the French go one better by calling the Witloof variety, described here, Chicorée endive, otherwise the plants described are known in France as Chicorée sauvage. The Italian red chicories come from *C. intybus*.

There are two main types of chicory grown: one looks rather similar to lettuce or endive according to variety and the other is the well-known Witloof or Brussels chicory. The first type is grown in a similar way to endive and readers are referred there for cultural details, though the two main varieties of it are given below; they do not require blanching however. The cultural details which follow here deal with the Witloof variety.

SOIL

Any good garden soil enriched with compost or manure for a previous crop and well dug in spring. At the same time, except on limy or chalky soils, add a sprinkling of carbonate of lime, about 6 oz to the square yard – weigh a handful to see how much you need to scatter.

SOW

April to May in rows and later thin out to about 9 inches apart.

CULTIVATION

Cultivation is in two main stages: first, to grow good roots; second, to force the roots from which the 'chicons' – the edible leaf shoots – grow. For the first stage, keep plants growing well by ensuring there is adequate moisture and that they are kept reasonably weed-free. Slugs may be attracted but the plants are generally pest and disease free. The second stage starts in October or November when the plants begin to die down. Lift the roots carefully, cutting off the foliage just above the crown. Then trim the roots to about 8 inches long and store them in a cool, frost-proof place.

CROP

As required, take a few of the stored roots at a time and place them upright in a suitable container – a large pot or a box will do – and pack them around with peat or sand. If they are not in a light-proof place cover them up to keep all light out by placing another pot or box on top. Put them in a warmer place and in 3 or 4 weeks, the chicons should be about 5 inches or more long and ready for cutting.

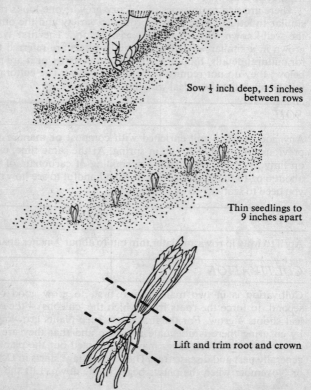

Sow ½ inch deep, 15 inches between rows

Thin seedlings to 9 inches apart

Lift and trim root and crown

RECOMMENDED VARIETIES

Witloof type: Witloof is the only readily available variety.
Lettuce types: Pain du Sucre/Sugar loaf – similar to a large cos
lettuce.
Red Verona – similar to a red curly endive.
For the cultivation of lettuce types see under Endive.

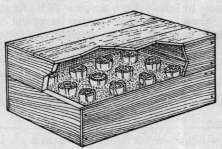

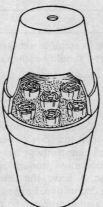

Place trimmed plants in
a box or pot packed with
peat or sand; keep light
out by covering with
another box or pot

Cut chicons when about
5 inches long

CHIVES

GENERAL

There are two types of chives: *Allium schoenoprasum* with pink-lilac flowers and hollow leaves, is the one usually grown; and *Allium tuberosum*, or Chinese chives, with white flowers and solid, flat leaves is slightly taller than the usual chives; but this is not a common plant in Britain. Both are perennials and may be used and grown in exactly the same way. The leaves and flower stems of both species provide a delicate onion flavour, though Chinese chives has the stronger of the two. The flower heads of both have the same onion flavour but with a taste of honey and are very decorative in salads. First-rate plants which are easily accommodated in the smallest of gardens.

SOIL

Any good, well-drained soil, in sun or semi-shade.

SOW OR PLANT

From autumn to spring in suitable weather. Seed of the common chive is also available and should be sown in March.

CULTIVATION

Transplant seedlings to their permanent positions, if not already sown there, in May. Keep plants moist during the growing season. It is recommended that flower heads should be pinched out; with newly-planted clumps those heads which are not eaten may be treated so to encourage production of more leaves. Once clumps are established, I leave the uneaten flower heads to flower – they are quite decorative. Large clumps may be split up in the autumn or spring and some can be potted up to grow on a window-sill indoors to provide leaves during the winter. Usually pest and disease-free.

CROP

As available and required from spring to when they die down.

RECOMMENDED VARIETIES

So far as I know there are no varieties of either species.

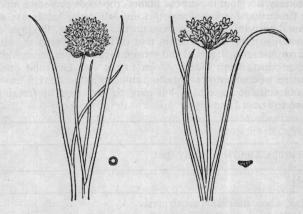

Common and Chinese chives

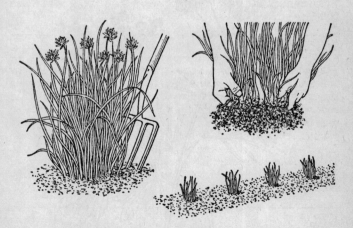

To propagate lift, divide and plant out,
if in rows about 9 inches apart

CORIANDER

GENERAL

Here truly is a double-purpose plant – the seeds provide a spice and flavouring for curry and pickling while the leaves are an essential herb for flavouring most curries. However, the taste of the seed is quite different from that of the leaf. Seeds are also used for flavouring liqueurs and vermouths and other commercial food products from North Africa to the Far East and other countries where there is an Arabian culinary influence. The leaves are not suitable for drying but may be preserved by freezing. Grows to about 2 feet high.

SOIL

Well drained and in a sunny spot.

SOW

Spring, where the plants are to grow.

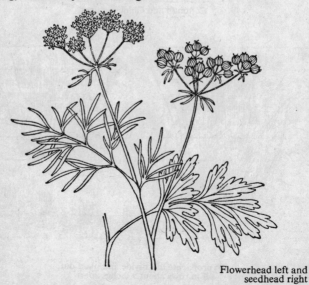

Flowerhead left and
seedhead right

Shaking the seeds free

CULTIVATION

Thin the seedlings to about 6 inches apart. Nine plants can be easily accommodated in about 18 inches square. Keep reasonably weed-free. Water in dry spells. Generally pest and disease-free but slugs may eat the seedlings and greenfly attack the growing plants.

CROP

Plants when nearly fully grown, but not seeding, should be stored by quickly freezing. Seeds when ripe in late summer to autumn should be dried.

RECOMMENDED VARIETIES

None.

CUCUMBER AND GHERKIN

GENERAL

Outdoor cucumbers have been improved, over the last few years, to such an extent that they can be grown as easily as marrows. Well not quite, perhaps, as they do seem to be a bit more susceptible to bad weather. However, the new varieties are long and succulent, very unlike the old stubby ridge cucumbers; one variety even states all its claims in its name – Burpless Tasty Green. Gherkins are treated in exactly the same way.

SOIL

Well-drained and well-manured in a sunny spot. Cucumbers may also be grown in tubs or growing bags of prepared peat.

SOW

Where they are to grow, from middle to end of May, watering in well. Some people recommend placing a glass jar over the seeds to assist germination.

CULTIVATION

Keep moist and well-watered in dry weather. When the cucumbers are a few inches long, feed weekly with liquid manure. Pinch out the growing tip when about 7 leaves have formed. Wood lice and slugs also may take a bite out of the fruits. Treat with BHC for the wood lice; slug killer for slugs around the fruit as well as

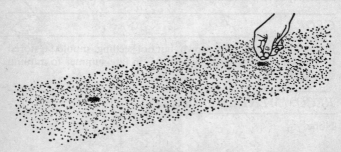

Sow some 3 feet apart

more widely around the plant. Remove and destroy any parts affected by *Botrytis* – grey mould.

CROP

Cucumbers when 9 to 12 inches long, summer and autumn; gherkins about 2 inches.

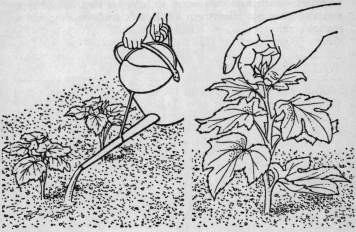

Keep well watered

Pinch out the growing tip when about 7 leaves have formed

Crop when 9–12 inches long

RECOMMENDED VARIETIES

Burpless Tasty Green F_1 – long.*
Nadir F_1 – long.
Chinese Long Green – long.
Burpee Hybrid F_1 – stubby.*

Gherkins – each seedsman seems to have his own named type and as I have not tried them all, I can't really recommend a particular one.

ENDIVE

GENERAL

For an attempt to explain the confusion over the naming of chicories and endives, see under Chicory. There are two generally available endive types – those with curled leaves (Chicorée frisée in France) and those with plain lettuce leaves (Chicorée scarole). Excellent salad plants, especially the late lettuce-leaved types which can be used when lettuce is scarcer.

SOIL

Well-manured. Later sowings can take over from a harvested crop for which the ground was liberally manured. Light soils are preferable but all soils should be well drained.

SOW

March to July for curly-leaved types and June to August for the lettuce-leaved types.

CULTIVATION

Keep well watered and weed-free. Not often troubled by pests or diseases. Blanch when large enough, only preparing a few at a time as the keeping quality deteriorates, by gathering the outer leaves over, making sure they are dry, and tying, preferably with raffia. Alternatively, blanch by placing a large pot, hole bunged up, or box, over the plants.

Curled leaved
endive

CROP

Blanching takes 7 to 14 days in summer and up to 21 later: crop when ready.

RECOMMENDED VARIETIES

Batavian Green – lettuce leaved.
Green Curled.

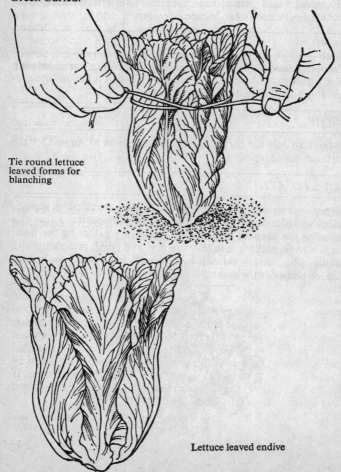

Tie round lettuce
leaved forms for
blanching

Lettuce leaved endive

FENNEL

GENERAL

The very ornamental foliage of this perennial plant makes it suitable for the flower border, and indeed there is a form grown and usually sold as a perennial for its decorative bronze foliage. Most families will only need a few plants. Be warned – it seeds itself freely and will grow some 6 feet or more high and has a considerable spread. The leaves provide a fine tangy taste for grilling with fish and for flavouring sauces and pickles. The seeds will flavour stews, sauces and soups, as well as pickles. Florence fennel is dealt with in the article following this. The fennels are closely related to the plant which provides the main source of anise seed and have something of the same flavour.

SOIL

Any reasonably fertile and well-draining soil. Will grow in a little shade but prefers full sun.

SOW

March to May. Only a few plants will usually be needed for the average family, so I think it's best to grow a corner clump, or have them in an ornamental border.

CULTIVATION

An easy-growing plant, perhaps too easy at times. Established plants should have the flower heads removed unless seed is required. If seed is the object, then I would recommend separate plants. For some reason, in my garden at any rate, greenfly are particularly attracted to the flower heads and they need repeated doses of insecticide to keep them free of the pests; this could be a nuisance if you want to use the leaves at the same time. If leaves are required during the winter, small plants may be potted and grown indoors on a window sill.

CROP

As required.

RECOMMENDED VARIETIES

Two colour forms are available, the common green and 'Golden' fennel. The latter is bronze in colour, and decorative.

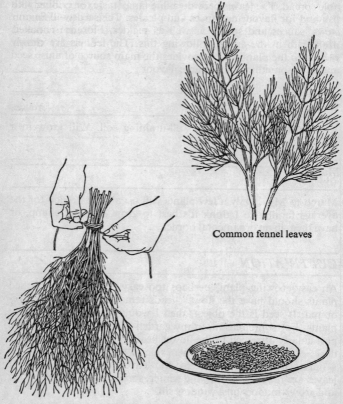

Common fennel leaves

Cut leaves being tied to hang for drying

Seeds shaken out on to a plate to dry

FENNEL, FLORENCE

GENERAL

The only way to appreciate fully all the uses of this plant is to grow it oneself. Greengrocers and supermarketeers sell only half the plant – what happens to the rest? The half that is easily obtainable consists of the swollen stem bases that distinguish this plant from the common fennel. But from the wasted half, both the leaves and the leaf stems are useful: the stems can be cooked like celery, and the leaves may be used as are those of the common fennel. The stem bases are delicious sliced raw in salads or cooked whole. The plant grows up to 2 feet in height. It is also known as finocchio.

SOIL

Well-drained, reasonably fertile, light and sandy for preference, and if possible in a sunny spot.

SOW

March and April where they are to grow.

Sow where you wish the plants to grow

CULTIVATION

Before sowing, add a sprinkling of a complete fertiliser such as Growmore. Keep watered, especially during dry weather, when growing. It is recommended that as the stem bases begin to swell, they should be earthed up or surrounded by paper collars to blanch them; but I don't. Slugs are fond of these bases and a slug killer should be used. I find the bran type the most effective. Otherwise, relatively pest and disease-free.

CROP

When the bases are sufficiently thick and swollen. Bits of leaf any time – leaves may be deep-frozen.

RECOMMENDED VARIETIES

None.

A maturing plant

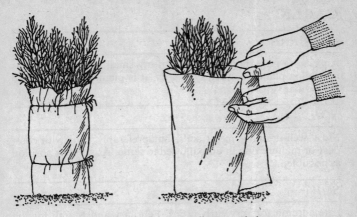

To blanch, wrap paper collar around plant

GARLIC

GENERAL

An easy-to-grow bulbous plant. In my small garden I use it as an edging plant. Remarkably hardy, it is planted and harvested before many other crops.

SOIL

Most well-draining moist soils, but preferably light with compost or manure dug in and allowed to settle. As sunny a position as possible.

SOW

Late autumn for very early crops. February and March for the main crop. Take the cloves off and plant them just below the soil, firming them well in. If any part is left showing, I find that birds will pull them out. Two bulbs will provide sufficient cloves for about 2 dozen new plants.

CULTIVATION

Keep weed-free and the bulbs themselves are usually trouble-free. Sometimes they are attacked by white rot – this fungus may be in the soil if you've grown onions. As a precaution, calomel dust should be applied before planting. Destroy infected bulbs.

A garlic bulb before separating   A separated clove

CROP

When the leaves die down, lift the bulbs and leave them to dry out in the sun. July and August.

RECOMMENDED VARIETIES

Obtain bulbs from a reliable source. Most reputable seedsmen sell garlic.

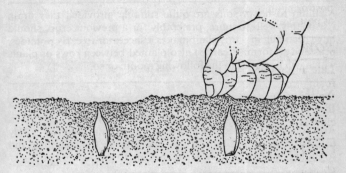

Plant cloves 6 inches apart with tips at ground level and firm

Lift to dry and mature when leaves yellow

KALE

GENERAL

A 'winter green' plant suitable for the coldest areas as it is extremely hardy. Curly kale, or borecole, is descriptive of the parsley-like leaves of many varieties. The flower heads of the variety 'Pentland Brig' can also be used as broccoli.

SOIL

Medium to heavy soils are quite suitable, provided they drain reasonably well. Manure, preferably for a previous crop, should have been dug in – this plant makes a successor to early potatoes, peas and so forth. It can be also planted between rows of plants which will be pulled in the following month or so.

SOW

Curly and plain-leaved kales are spring sown in a seed bed in April or May, thinned out as necessary and transplanted in July to final growing position. Rape kales dislike transplanting and so should be sown directly where they are to grow.

CULTIVATION

Keep as weed-free as practicable. Rarely really troubled by diseases or pests, though flea beetles may make the young plants look rather ragged by eating out holes in the leaves.

CROP

Mainly late winter to spring but leaves can be harvested from about December. Start by taking the centre out to encourage more tender growths to form at the stem below.

RECOMMENDED VARIETIES

Dwarf Green Curled (curly leaved).*
Hungry Gap (rape) – late.
Pentland Brig (crossed curly and plain leaved).*
Thousand Head(ed) (plain leaved).

Sow kale ¾ inch deep in rows 15 inches apart

Pinching out to encourage
side growths

Types of kale from curled to plain leaved

LEEK

GENERAL

Apart from its uses in Wales, the leek is an excellent vegetable, providing a change from the cabbage family when little else is available fresh. If you transplant, remember the surplus plants are extremely good to eat raw in a salad or cooked. May be grown as a border edging in small gardens; it reaches its greatest height during the winter months.

SOIL

Well-drained, well-dug with manure or compost added. Plots used for earlier salad crops or peas can be used.

SOW

Sow in a prepared seed bed, March and April. Transplant June and July. Unless you really want to exhibit rather than eat them, there is no need to dig massive trenches; instead, make holes up to 12 inches deep with a dibber or crowbar, and drop the seedlings in when they are 6 to 9 inches high. Trim the tops off the leaves at almost soil level – this encourages root growth.

Dibbing in leeks 6–12 inches deep

CULTIVATION

A few weeks before planting out, add a little lime to soils if they are acid, and on all sorts scatter a sprinkling of fish manure or Growmore on top. When the seedlings have been put in the holes, water them in. Keep well watered until properly established.

CROP

According to variety from September to March.

RECOMMENDED VARIETIES

Lyon (Prizetaker), Abel – early.*
Musselburgh – mid-season.
Winter Crop – late.

Trimming leek tops after planting

A dibber may be made from the broken-off handle of a garden tool

LETTUCE

GENERAL

If you like your lettuce to be young, sweet and crisp, then this is really a vegetable for home growing. Moreover by growing your own you may enjoy varieties rarely, if ever, seen in the shops – especially the small and compact ones. Lettuces can be grown out of doors more or less the whole year round. Concerning successive sowings in spring and summer, however, I have found that most lettuces try to arrive at the same time, the later sowings doing their best to catch up with the first. Therefore, as an alternative I try to get successions going by transplanting – I sow half a row at the beginning of April, and thin out later, replanting some of the thinnings, and thin again later to leave the sown row to crop and again replant some of the thinnings. This works well with Webbs Wonderful, Tom Thumb and Little Gem or Sugar Cos but may cause premature bolting. Salad Bowl is a non-hearting variety which produces lots of straggling leaves, which can be picked as required. It became quite a rage at one time but it has little to recommend growing it.

Sow lettuce successionally

Thin out to 9–12 inches apart

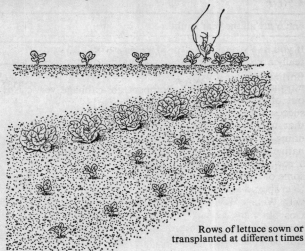

Rows of lettuce sown or
transplanted at different times

SOIL

Well-drained, especially if growing winter and spring cropping lettuce. Preferably, the soil should have been manured for a previous crop and lightened, if necessary, with peat or compost.

SOW

Where they are to grow. March to early August, for summer and autumn crops. August and September for spring crops. Check you have the right variety for sowing at the right time.

CULTIVATION

Plenty of water, and that also means good weeding to prevent the lettuce being robbed. Slugs and leatherjackets enjoy lettuce; birds especially when suffering (or enjoying?) spring fever are apt to rip and tear the leaves – otherwise there is little that is likely to bother the amateur except the greenfly in overwinter crops; spraying with Malathion should deal with this.

CROP

Virtually all the year round.

RECOMMENDED VARIETIES

Spring-summer sown:
   Little Gem/Sugar Cos – compact, cos-cabbage, very crisp†
   Tom Thumb – compact, cabbage, crisp†
   Webbs Wonderful – large, crisp
Spring or autumn sown:
   Winter Density – crisp, cos-cabbage
Autumn sown:
   Imperial Winter – large, cabbage

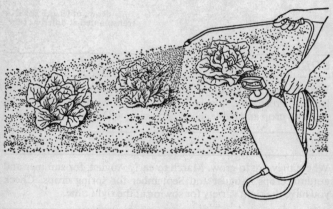

Spraying overwinter lettuce to
keep aphids in check

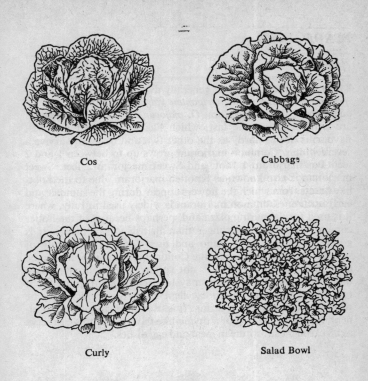

Cos

Cabbage

Curly

Salad Bowl

Types of lettuce

MARJORAM

GENERAL

There are three marjorams generally available in Britain; Common or wild marjoram, *Origanum vulgare*; Pot marjoram, *O. onites*; and Sweet marjoram, *O. majorana*. All three marjorams are perennials but the last, which has the sweetest and best flavour, is not as hardy as the other two and may not survive a severe winter. Common marjoram grows up to between 1 and 2 feet, Pot marjoram 1 foot, and Sweet marjoram 2 feet. Sweet marjoram is also known as Knotted marjoram, due to the knot-like bracts from which the flowers appear during the summer and early autumn. Common marjoram is widely used in Italy, where it is used for flavouring pizza and, perhaps because of the hotter climate, seems much stronger than British grown plants. It is generally known as Oregano and used for a wide variety of strongly flavoured dishes on the Continent. Pot marjoram can be used in a similar way but is not so strong and, though more bitter than Sweet marjoram, may be used as a substitute for it too. Sweet marjoram is an excellent green herb which may be preserved by drying or freezing. It is used throughout the Continent, having something of a thyme-like flavour and this can serve as an excellent substitute in meat and egg dishes.

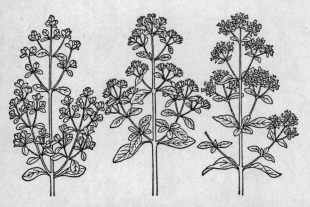

Types of marjoram: Sweet, Pot and Common

SOIL

A sunny spot with well-drained soil.

SOW

Seed in April; cuttings planted indoors April to May, are transplanted, after hardening off, in May. Seed can also be started in pots indoors February to March and transplanted, after hardening off, in May.

CULTIVATION

Apart from keeping reasonably weed-free and trimming if they spread too much, marjorams are little trouble to grow.

Marjoram may be grown
in pots or in the border

CROP

Leaves as required; plants in the late summer for drying, or for freezing the leaves.

RECOMMENDED VARIETIES

No real culinary varieties but the Common marjoram has a yellow-leaved form known as *Origanum vulgare* 'Aureum'.

MARROW AND COURGETTE

GENERAL

Thank goodness that the days have gone when a slice of marrow would engulf a dinner plate. Young, small marrows are tender and delicious. Moreover there is a variation in flavour between different types. Most of us know the taste of vegetable marrow and more people are becoming aware of the excellence of courgettes or zucchini; the richer flavoured custard marrows are worthwhile trying and so is the vegetable spaghetti. The latter is best cooked whole, and that means harvesting it when it is of a size to fill the saucepan, and simmering for twenty to thirty minutes in water brought to the boil. It can then be cut in two and the insides forked out like strings of spaghetti; eaten hot with butter, the strings are quite unusual, but they can also be left to cool and eaten cold with salads. A recent introduction is the yellow courgette which can be eaten, like other courgettes, raw or cooked but it does not always seem to grow as successfully in colder seasons. My palate is not distinguished enough to tell any difference in flavour and the green courgettes, boiled for two or three minutes, drained and then rolled in butter, are still excellent. Another unusual courgette is 'Aristocrat' on which the fruits tend to point upwards. The trailing types of marrow have no advantage that I can see over the bush types, indeed they have a positive disadvantage in taking up a great deal more space, and that may be very important in smaller gardens. Generally speaking, and unless the weather is absolutely foul, marrows of all types are easy to grow, and also, kept regularly cropped, prolific.

SOIL

You may grow marrows on heaps of rotting compost: but that

Prepare site by digging and adding compost

puts the compost out of action for anything else. Much easier, and less likely to cause watering or rotting problems, is to grow them on a flat, but dug, bed in which the plant sites have been enriched with farmyard or horse manure, compost or a peat and fish manure mixture. The important thing is that the sites must be able to retain moisture and feed the plants gently. Warmth is also important and a sunny position the best.

Sow seeds
individually in
peat pots

Plant out the plant and peat pot to avoid disturbance

SOW

Germination is usually good and, although some people recommend sowing two or three seeds per pot or where the plants are to grow, I sow one. If there is a failure, it is easy enough to put another seed in, and such later sowings catch up pretty well with the earlier ones. If sowing indoors, use 3 inch peat pots, April

88

to May. Sow outside directly where the plants are to grow, mid-May to early June. Indoor sowings will provide plants earlier than outdoors but generally only make a week or two's difference in cropping times.

CULTIVATION

Transplant indoor sowings late May. Keep reasonably weed-free and moist. Plants are usually pretty trouble-free from a gardener's point of view. However slugs enjoy the plants, especially when young, and should be dealt with. Sometimes the fruits rot at the end, more often when the weather is cold and damp. Rotten fruit should be destroyed to prevent infection of others. Overwatering will also tend to cause fruit rot. If you grow trailing types it is best to pinch out the main shoot when it is about 18 inches long; this induces the growth of lateral shoots which bear predominantly female, hence fruiting, flowers.

CROP

Regularly, the younger the better; regular cropping keeps the plants fruiting longer. The last fruits can be left to finish growing and ripening on the plant until late autumn, picked and stored in a dry place for winter use; the outsides become very tough and the insides a mere shadow of a young, fresh marrow.

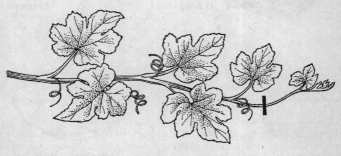

Pinch out to stop

RECOMMENDED VARIETIES

Trailing marrows:

1 { Long Green.
  { Long White.

2 Vegetable Spaghetti.

3 Little Gem (small, rich fruit).

Bush marrows:

1 or 4 Green Bush (can be used for courgette production).

4 Aristocrat (can be used for courgette production).

4 Zucchini (can be used for courgette production).

5 Custard White.

3 Golden Nugget (small, rich fruit).

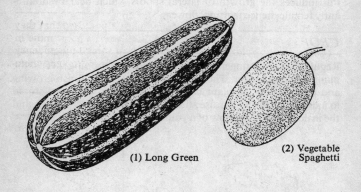

(1) Long Green

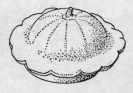

(2) Vegetable Spaghetti

(3) Golden Nugget

(4) Courgette

(5) Custard White

MINT

GENERAL

Probably the most commonly cultivated culinary mint is the Spearmint with longish, willow-like leaves. Though it has a sharp minty flavour it is not as 'minty' as Apple mint or as French (Bowles) mint. Spearmint grows about 2 feet in height; Apple mint grows about 2 to 3 feet high and has light green, hairy and rounded leaves; French mint, a hybrid between Apple mint and Spearmint, grows to about 3 feet or more. Its leaves are larger than Apple mint and are darker green and not so hairy on the upper surfaces. To me, this is the most satisfactory of these three mints.

SOIL

Mints may be rampant growers and, though it is advised that they should be grown in well-dug and manured soils, I grow mine in shade and among shrubs where their natural spreading tendency is restricted. They may also be grown in containers to keep them in bounds.

SOW

Plant the roots horizontally just below the surface of the soil in spring.

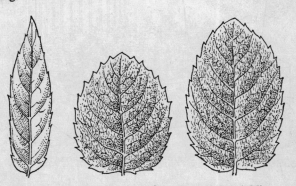

Types of mint: Spearmint, Apple Mint and French Mint

CULTIVATION

Apart from keeping young plants reasonably weed-free and moist, little attention is required. They are generally pest-free but rust may attack the plants. It is then best to destroy the plants and start afresh, in another position with new roots which may be taken from the infected plant. From late autumn, roots may be potted up, at intervals, to provide mint from the kitchen window-sill.

CROP

As required.

RECOMMENDED VARIETIES

As mentioned above under General.

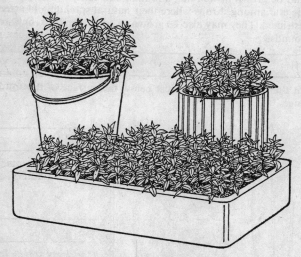

Mint may be grown in various containers

ONION

GENERAL

Basically onions are used in three main ways. First, 'spring' onions, which can be sown as late as July, making the name somewhat suspect, and which may be grown from seed, or from divisions of the 'Welsh' onion, or be provided by shallots. Second, as pickling onions – again shallots provide an excellent substitute. Third for cooking, and for some purposes the shallot again is a substitute – especially in stews. The Welsh onion, also known as Ciboule, is rather like a large chive plant, and while the leaves can be used in much the same way as chive leaves, it is really grown as a perpetual spring onion. It should be planted and divided in March or April. There are other types of onion but they are not easy to get hold of.

When dealing with the main onion type, you must decide whether to grow from seed or sets. Seed is, or course, essential for the production of spring or salad onions; it may also provide the best onions, if you do not live in cold and rather wet areas, and if you have the extra time and space to grow them. Sets are the easiest and the most convenient way of growing onions, especially for small gardens where quicker-maturing crops help to keep up the all-round productivity. There is therefore no point in considering onions from seed, except to provide spring onions – other publications deal with the production of exhibition produce.

SOIL

A well-cultivated, previously manured, and friable soil in a sunny site is best. Heavy soils should be broken up with the addition of compost or peat and some sand.

SOW

Sets are the small onions, readily available in the early spring for planting. They should be placed in firmed soil with sufficient to cover the swollen bulb. The wisp of last year's died-down shoots is best removed, or if not too long, bent over and covered too;

this prevents birds, which in this respect can be a great nuisance, plucking the bulbs out and chucking them about. Having planted, trample the bulbs in, then water well.

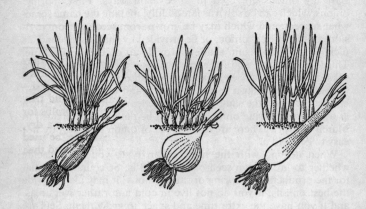

Types of onion: Welsh or Everlasting, Shallot, Spring, Maincrop Flat and Round

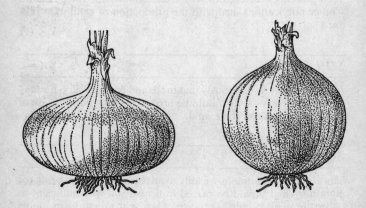

CULTIVATION

Keep as weed-free as possible and water in dry weather – do not overwater. Onion fly can be a nuisance and the soil should be treated at planting time with calomel dust.

CROP

When the leaves start drying off and the bulbs colour up – they will then be growing above ground – lift them and lay them down along the rows to dry off. Three or four weeks may be needed – the larger the bulbs the longer it takes to ripen them, and they should be turned two or three times to ripen all round. Bulbs for storing should be tied up by the dried leaves and hung in a dry, cool and airy place. The legs of ladies' tights can also be used successfully – place a bulb in, knot and repeat until full and then hang the tight leg up in a dry, frost-free place.

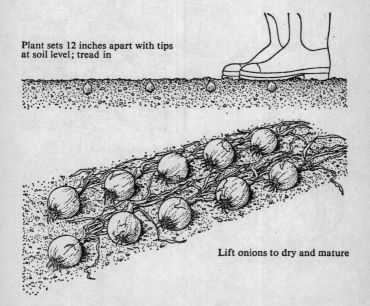

Plant sets 12 inches apart with tips at soil level; tread in

Lift onions to dry and mature

RECOMMENDED VARIETIES

White Lisbon – for spring onions.
Stuttgarter Giant – sets.
Rijnsburger Wijbo – heat-prepared sets. †
Sturon – a new variety, sets.
Red – flat, mild, from seed.

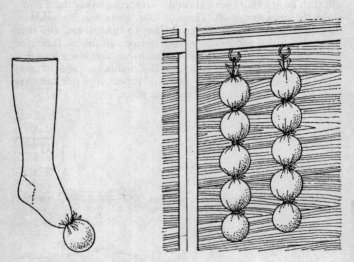

Onions may be stored in discarded stockings

PARSLEY

GENERAL

This is an excellent herb – the stems are as good as the leaves for flavour but, of course, not as decorative sprinkled over salads. It is a plant that may be grown as an edging, 9 to 18 inches high, and left to sow itself here and there. Indeed, I have needed to sow parsley only twice in ten years. However if you do not want it to sow itself, remove the bud clusters before they flower – they may be eaten too. Parsley flavour may vary according to the climate and soil. Parsley seeds in its second year and then dies as it is a biennial plant. It is curious that here we grow almost exclusively the curly-leaved varieties while on the Continent the plain-leaved is preferred. There is also a parsley grown for its root and known as Turnip-rooted or Hamburg parsley. The leaves of Hamburg parsley are not of quite so good a flavour as the ordinary parsley, but the root is something between parsnip and celeriac in flavour though turnip-like in shape.

SOIL

A sheltered position will help provide winter needs with a well-drained soil in sun or semi-shade. Grows more vigorously if the soil has been enriched with well-decayed manure or compost.

SOW

Where it is to grow as an edging plant or as a patch, otherwise in rows, February to June, or straight into a window box. Hamburg in rows, March to April.

Seedhead

CULTIVATION

Little is needed except to thin out the seedlings and keep as weed-free as possible. Water in hot or dry weather. Generally pretty pest and disease-free for the gardener.

CROP

Ordinary parsley as required. Pot up a few plants to keep going on a window-sill through winter. Hamburg parsley from October. May be lifted and stored in a dry, cool but frost-free place.

RECOMMENDED VARIETIES

Ordinary – there are a number of varieties of very similar quality offered by different seedsmen: a reliable seedsmen will offer reliable seed.
Hamburg – Turnip Rooted (there is only the one).

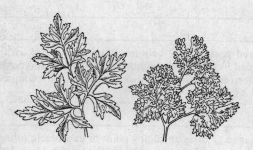

Leaf types: plain and curled

Parsley may be grown as an attractive edging to a border

PARSNIP

GENERAL

Easy to grow but not particularly good for the small garden as they have a long growing season.

SOIL

As the plants have long roots, parsnip beds should be well dug. Fresh manure should not be used as the root will fork, if it is. The soil should preferably have been manured for a previous crop and be in an open site.

SOW

February to May. As the seeds are fairly large they may be sown singly at about 4 inch intervals.

Sow 1 inch deep, 4 inches apart in rows 18 inches apart

Thin to at least 8 inches apart

CULTIVATION

Thin the seedlings – whether sown singly or freely – to a minimum of 8 inches apart. Keep weed-free if you can. Canker may be a problem – brown to blackish patches appear round the top of the root and cause rotting. There are no generally recognised control measures, some say limy loam will help but others maintain that late sowings – those sown April to May – suffer less. Celery fly may damage leaves but pests are rarely a bother.

CROP

When the leaves die down in the autumn and through the winter as required. They can also be lifted and stored in boxes of slightly damp sand in a cool but frost-free place, but they do tend to keep better in the ground.

RECOMMENDED VARIETIES

Avonresister – resists canker.
Tender and True – also has some resistance to canker.

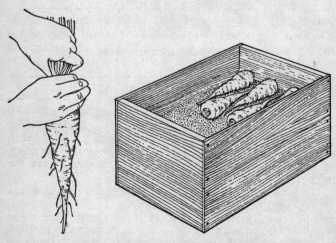

Parsnips may be stored in boxes or in a clamp

PEA

GENERAL

There are several unusual peas, the Asparagus pea, the Mange-tout or sugar pea, and even a purple-podded pea, which are well worth trying – especially as they are virtually impossible to buy from a greengrocer. They may all be grown in the same way as the ordinary garden pea though the Asparagus pea belongs to a different genus. It has pods with four wrinkled wings and should be picked at 1½ to 2 inches long, before it fills out and toughens. Similarly the Mangetout, which means 'eat all', is grown for its pod which is picked flat. The purple-podded pea is excellent for eating either uncooked when young or as a dried pea, but is otherwise used like an ordinary garden pea; it has green peas inside the purple pods.

Ordinary garden peas come in two main types, round-seeded and wrinkle-seeded. The round-seeded ones are hardier and so more suitable for sowing early and late in the year; they generally are not quite as sweet or as heavy-cropping as the wrinkle-seeded types.

SOIL

Well-dug, well-draining and well-manured, a couple of buckets of well-rotted compost or manure should be dug in per square yard. Some growers add a general fertiliser, as well, raking in 2 or 3 oz to the square yard a week or so before sowing.

SOW

In flat-bottomed shallow trenches 2 to 3 inches deep and 4 to 6 inches wide. Aim to get about 8 peas alternately placed at either side per foot. Asparagus pea I sow singly into a V-shaped trench and cover. Space trenches at the same distance apart as the height of the variety – which should be given on the seed packet. See recommended varieties for sowing times.

CULTIVATION

Keep well-watered in dry weather and as weed-free as possible. Stake with twigs or support with netting to the appropriate height. A tall row of peas can offer considerable wind resistance, so if using netting make sure that it is well-supported with stout stakes. A large list of pests and diseases which might affect peas may be compiled but there are few to be wary about: maggot-like caterpillars of pea moths bore little holes into the young pods and feed on the peas; the eggs are laid on the leaves in the summer and so early sowing, for up to July harvesting, and late sowings after June, will generally be free of the pests; slugs and sparrows may worry young plants and should be treated with a slug killer, and black threads stretched about the rows respectively: none of the diseases should be cause for concern.

Sow ordinary
peas in a double row
4–6 inches wide and
2–3 inches deep

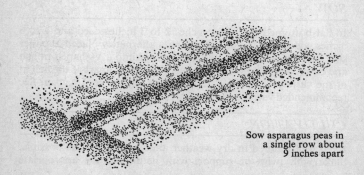

Sow asparagus peas in
a single row about
9 inches apart

CROP

Pick as soon as ready to ensure maximum cropping, like beans, for leaving mature pods on the plants may discourage production.

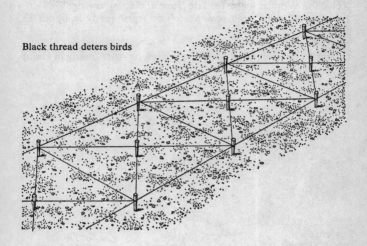

Black thread deters birds

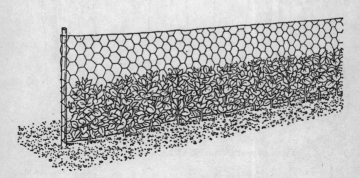

Chicken wire provides a good support for ordinary peas

RECOMMENDED VARIETIES

Ordinary garden peas: for early cropping, sow March or April, ready in about 12 weeks.

Early Onward.

Feltham First – also for late (June and July) sowing.

Kelvedon Wonder – also for late (June and July) sowing.

For mid-cropping peas, sow March or April, ready in about 13 weeks.

Hurst Green Shaft.

Onward – late-cropping peas, sow March or April, ready in about 14 or 15 weeks.

Dwarf Greensleaves.

Recette.

Latest cropping peas, sow June or July, see early cropping above.

Unusual peas: Mangetout – Sugar dwarf de Grace.

        Purple-podded.

        Asparagus.

        Petit Pois – Gullivert.

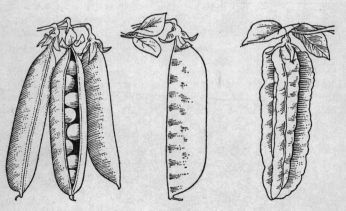

Types of pea: Ordinary, Mangetout and Asparagus

POTATO

GENERAL

I think that the potato suffers somewhat from what might be called the 'marrow complex' – quantity rather than quality being the criterion. However, if you do have enough ground it is worth growing the smaller, but delicious, types such as 'Fir Apple', if you can get them. They are sometimes known as French potatoes. Such varieties retain the fresh new potato taste throughout the season and are excellent cooked, and cooled for salads. Fir Apple in particular may have very odd-shaped and knobbly roots – so if you grow them for the first time don't necessarily think some terrible disease has struck. Personally, I would not grow the larger types if short of space, except for early new potatoes as they are so readily available throughout the year. Potatoes, however, benefit the ground for they clear and clean it of weeds and break it up into a good loam for future cultivations.

SOIL

Potatoes can be grown on nearly all soils but plenty of humus should be added to both sandy and clay soils in the autumn, using well-rotted manure or compost for preference. The ground should then be left as dug to let it weather by frost, rain and sun.

SOW

Buy the 'seed' potatoes, small tubers, early in the year and put them on trays or in boxes in a frost-free, but cool, light place. When they sprout, leave only the two best shoots to grow when planting. The first potatoes, the earlies and second earlies, may be planted from March to April according to your locality – the earlier times for southern sheltered areas; main crop varieties April. To provide new potatoes for the summer and autumn, planting can go on until late June or even the beginning of July. Remember that the quicker growing earlies take about three months to mature and main-crop about four. Plant each tuber in a hole about 5 inches deep in rows 2 feet apart; the tubers should be spaced at 12 inches for earlies and second earlies, and 3 inches more for main crop. Cover with soil. When the shoots appear, soil may be drawn up around them, forming ridges along

105

the rows about 6 or 7 inches high. The main pest is Potato Cyst eelworm and amateurs should avoid concentrations of this soil-borne pest by regular rotation. Diseases are better known and include Potato Blight and Potato Wart. Potato Blight is a fungal disease which shows as brown spots on the leaves which may shrivel up completely and die; spray affected plants with a suitable copper, zinc or manganese based fungicide. Potato Wart is a less common but more serious disease. Warty outgrowth appears, especially around the eyes, and if suspected report it to the Ministry of Agriculture. There are plenty of varieties of potato which are immune to the disease. Scab also appears on the surface of the tubers, rather blotchy, irregular patches which are generally more disfiguring than troublesome. Soils poor in organic materials seem to give rise to these scabs – so add as much organic material as you can unless you grow a scab resistant variety.

Seed potatoes sprouting and ready for planting out

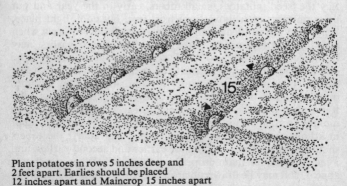

Plant potatoes in rows 5 inches deep and
2 feet apart. Earlies should be placed
12 inches apart and Maincrop 15 inches apart

As required. During October the main crop potatoes may be lifted and stored. Cut down the top growth a few weeks before lifting; this helps reduce the incidence of disease spores 'taking'. A storage clamp is made by lining a shallow trench with a few inches of straw which is then heaped with potatoes up to about 3 feet high. Cover this with straw about 6 inches thick and then the same amount of soil. Ventilation is essential and twists of straw pushed in every few feet will provide this.

Earthing up

Diseases: Blight, Wart disease and Scab

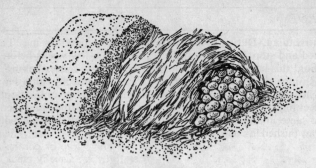

How a clamp is made up

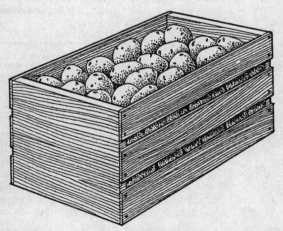

Potatoes may be stored in a box if they are to be used quickly

RECOMMENDED VARIETIES

It pays to find out what grows best in your area from local gardeners; or at least, since there will almost certainly be several recommendations, you might find out what you should not grow.

Earlies: Suttons' Foremost, Arran Pilot.

Second Earlies: Craig's Royal.

Main crop: Majestic, King Edward, Red King.

108

RADISH

GENERAL

Radishes are among the easiest of plants to grow but make sure that they grow quickly – plenty of water if the weather does not provide it – or else they will become hot and will go quickly to seed without swelling the root. There are two main types grown: the ordinary salad radish which is round, stump or long-rooted and the winter radish which is either round or long-rooted. The former comes in shades of pink, carmine and white or combinations of the two, and also yellow: the latter are usually black or pink carmine and comparatively very large, maybe a pound in weight, and virtually impossible to eat whole; they are best sliced into strips. Long-rooted salad radishes are best avoided on heavy stony soils where they will tend to fork.

SOIL

Good soil prepared with well-rotted compost or manure is best and in a moist position.

SOW

Ordinary salad radishes may be sown from about March to September. Short rows, successively sown, provide radishes for five or six months. Along a 6 foot row and in a width of about 15 inches you can sow some 5 successional rows; that equals a 30 foot row. The large winter radishes need more space between rows, about 9 inches, and the best time to sow is July to early August.

CULTIVATION

Thin seedlings of salad radishes to prevent spindly growth, caused by overcrowding, and to allow the roots to swell. Keep them moist and as weed-free as you can. Winter radishes should be thinned to about 6 inches apart and if you sow in adjacent rows, the rows should be about 9 inches apart. Pests are not usually much trouble, the flea beetle makes unsightly holes in the leaves, while slugs may do their usual damage to seedlings and roots.

The former may be controlled by spraying Derris or BHC and the latter checked by a slug killer. Diseases are not usually any bother.

HARVEST

Salad varieties as ready and required – they will toughen if left too long in the soil. Winter varieties when ready – they can be left in the ground into the winter but in very severe weather may require protection by a covering such as straw. They may also be lifted and stored, by placing them in boxes of sand in a cool but airy place.

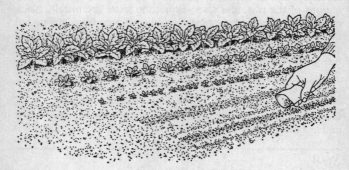

Sow successional rows

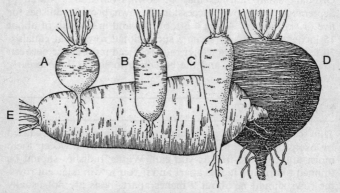

Types of radish: (a) turnip-rooted salad, (b) stump salad, (c) long salad, (d) round black Spanish and (e) China Rose

Salad: mixed varieties from a well-known seedsman should provide interest in colour and are usually of the round, turnip-rooted types.

round – Cherry Belle – bright red

       Saxa Red Prince – bright scarlet, large.†

stump – French Breakfast – red, white tipped.

long – Long White Icicle (Icicle) – white and of good flavour.†

Winter: China (Chinese) Rose – deep pink, long rooted.

Black Spanish Long – black, long rooted.

Black Spanish Round – black, large round rooted.

ROSEMARY

GENERAL

This is a fine evergreen shrub which holds its own in any shrub border as a decorative plant, as well as providing an excellent herb. It may also be grown in tubs or large pots. As a herb it is used for flavouring meat, try it when grilling, fish and fowl. The plants cultivated are forms of *Rosmarinus officinalis* which is found wild in Southern Europe, and are not a hundred percent hardy, especially in damp positions.

SOIL

Well-drained, even on the dry side rather than too moist, and in a sunny position. While the soil should have some goodness in it, rosemary will tolerate a poorer soil than most culinary plants.

SOW

September to March, where they can be left to grow in a sunny border, either in the kitchen garden or flower garden. Dig a hole just larger than the pot it comes in, take it out of its pot and place the plant in the hole, fill in with soil and firm in by hand.

CULTIVATION

Apart from making sure it does not suffer from undue lack of moisture in dry weather when establishing itself in its new position, the plant should not require attention. Straggly shoots may be removed if a nuisance. New plants may be raised by taking mature shoots, 6 or 7 inches long, in the early autumn or spring, and planting them directly where they are to grow. Treat as for plants planted from pots. Pests and diseases are unlikely to cause trouble. Late frosts however may damage shoots turning them partially or even completely brown.

CROP

All the year round.

There are a few forms of the species including some which grow more upright, such as 'Jessop's Upright'. They are no different from the culinary point of view though the intensity of the violet blue flowers may differ slightly.

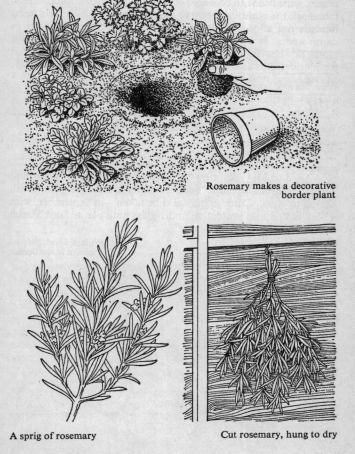

Rosemary makes a decorative
border plant

A sprig of rosemary

Cut rosemary, hung to dry

SAGE

GENERAL

Sage besides being useful as an evergreen herb is a decorative garden plant and, because of this, it may be conveniently grown in a border as an edging plant in front of shrubs or as a specimen plant. Botanically named *Salvia officinalis*, the common sage has several varieties with coloured leaves adding to its attractiveness; but check the plants you buy to make sure that they have a good flavour, not all do. It is not always hardy either, especially in damp areas. It blooms in the summer, carrying small bluish violet flowers. In the kitchen its aromatic leaves may be used fresh or dried to add flavour to most meat dishes, soups, poultry, sausages and stuffing.

SOIL

Well-drained and light, in full sun if possible.

SOW

Sow April to May, planting the seedlings into their final position when a reasonable size: bought plants should be planted in March to April. Cuttings may also be taken – in September, with a heel, but require protection under glass until planted out March to April.

Another plant which may be grown in the border

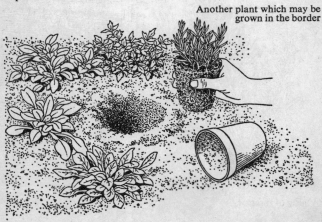

CULTIVATION

Keep clear of weeds, and also other plants until well-established in a border. Pinch out flowers to encourage leaf growth – the flavour is considered by some best before flowering. Usually trouble-free from pests and diseases.

CROP

As required.

RECOMMENDED VARIETIES

There are purple, yellow and variegated leaved varieties, but the common sage probably has the best flavour.

Sage shoots

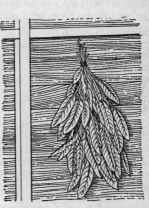

Sage hung to dry

SALSIFY

GENERAL

Although salsify is a biennial plant, taking two years for its full cycle from seed to seeding, it is grown as an annual for its roots. These are long and said by some to possess something of an oyster-like flavour. Although it takes about five months or so to develop good roots these may be left in the ground over winter and used as required. They may be cooked either by boiling and serving with butter, or by frying slices in butter. Botanically named *Tragopogon porrifolius*, it belongs to the same genus as our native Goat's Beard, *T. pratensis*.

SOIL

As salsify has long roots, the soil should be well-dug and as many stones removed as possible. The soil should be light for preference and have been manured or composted for a previous crop.

SOW

April, $\frac{1}{2}$ to 1 inch deep in drills 12 to 15 inches apart.

CULTIVATION

Thin seedlings to about 9 inches apart. Keep weed-free and well-watered. Usually pest and disease-free, though the descriptively named White blister fungal disease may appear attacking the leaves – cut them off if they offend you but the disease is unlikely to cripple.

CROP

From about October through the winter.

RECOMMENDED VARIETIES

Few varieties have been developed but 'Sandwich Island' has large, sweet roots.

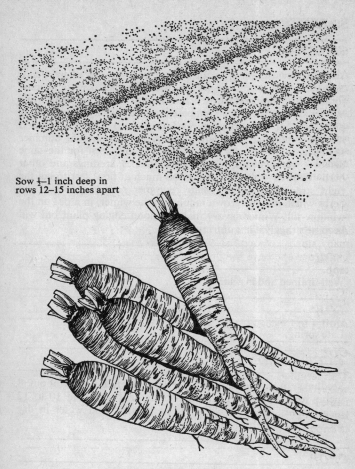

Sow ½–1 inch deep in
rows 12–15 inches apart

Salsify roots prepared for the kitchen

SAVORY

GENERAL

There are two main types of savory, both species of the genus *Satureja* which is related to the mints, thymes, sage and marjorams. The Summer savory *S. hortensis*, is an annual, while Winter savory *S. montana* is a perennial, semi-evergreen, shrubby plant. Both are easy to grow, reaching about 1 foot in height and having something of a sage flavour, but the annual Summer savory is said to be the finer. They are both used for the same dishes – soups, beans, meat and fish dishes, stuffings and other herb mixtures – but do not use too much at first; test to get the right strength for your palate. Summer savory is one of the herbs which may be grown indoors in the winter, in a pot on the window-sill. Winter savory makes a good edging plant but will become straggly if left untrimmed.

SOIL

Well-drained and in a sunny spot.

SOW

Late spring.

CULTIVATION

Seedlings of Summer savory should be thinned to about 8 inches apart and the plants of Winter savory spaced 10 to 12 inches apart. Keep as weed-free as possible and water in dry weather until established.

CROP

As required. Summer savory may be dried – choose the shoots before flowering on a dry day and hang bunches in a warm, dry and airy place, preferably in the shade. Make sure that they are completely dry before storing in jars.

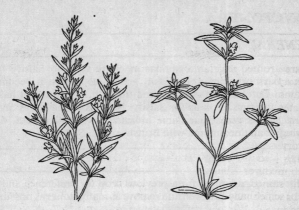

Types of savory: Winter and Summer

Winter savory should be planted 10–12 inches
apart and Summer savory 8 inches apart

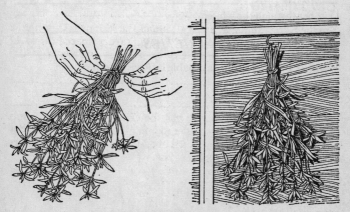

Summer savory may be cut and dried for later use

SCORZONERA

GENERAL

A long rooted vegetable, similar in many ways to Salsify but with a dark brownish skin. Easily grown, as Salsify, it becomes ready in October and may be used through the winter. It has a delicate flavour. Cook as for Salsify. Belongs to the genus *Scorzonera*, as its vernacular name indicates; the cultivated *S. hispanica* has an uncommon, wild British cousin, *S. humilis*.

SOIL

Well-drained, manured for a previous crop for preference and in sun or semi-shade. Dig well and remove as many stones as possible.

SOW

Late spring, $\frac{1}{2}$ inch deep, in rows.

CULTIVATION

Thin seedlings to about 10 inches apart. Keep weed-free and watered.

CROP

October through the winter.

RECOMMENDED VARIETIES

Virtually the only variety available is 'Russian Giant'.

Sow ½ inch deep

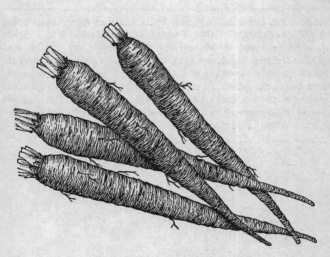

Scorzonera roots ready for the kitchen

SHALLOT

GENERAL

These easy-to-grow plants, closely related to the onion, may be used in a variety of ways – as spring onions, pickling onions and are excellent in stews. The exhibition varieties, where single large bulbs are required, are hardly worth the bother to the kitchen gardener and are therefore not discussed here. Needing an open and sunny spot, they make good, though temporary, edgings to beds used mainly for other purposes.

SOIL

Reasonably good and well-drained soil, manured or composted for a previous crop, in a sunny position.

SOW

Shallots are not usually grown from seed but from small bulbs which are readily available. They should be planted 6 to 7 inches apart in February to March. The tips of the bulbs should be at soil level. Long dead tips may be trimmed but beware you do not also trim the growing point. Firm them well in, as some birds seem to take a delight in tossing them out. If grown in adjacent rows, the rows should be about 1 foot apart or the shallots should be staggered 9 inches apart and 9 inches between rows.

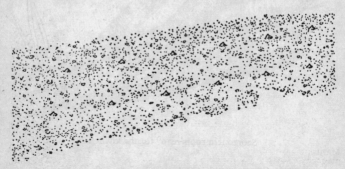

Plant shallots firmly, 6–7 inches apart,
with the tips just at soil level

CULTIVATION

Keep reasonably weed-free and moist as they grow. Usually pest and disease-free but onion fly may be troublesome: dust the plot with calomel at planting time.

CROP

As spring onions when clusters have formed. For keeping, wait until the leaves turn yellow, lift and leave the clumps to ripen and dry off. Turn for a few days to ensure even drying. Separate the bulbs and store.

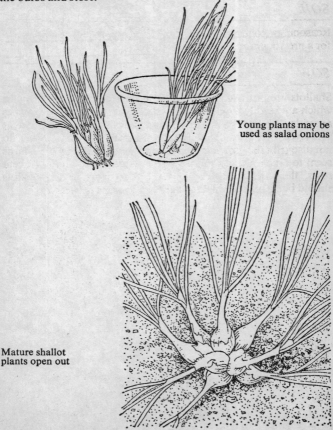

Young plants may be used as salad onions

Mature shallot plants open out

RECOMMENDED VARIETIES

Dutch Yellow – Longkeeping Yellow.
Dutch Red – Longkeeping Red.

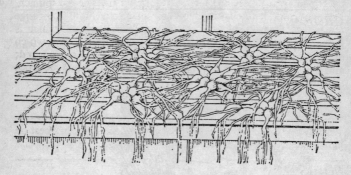

Shallots drying out

SPINACH

GENERAL

There are several plants now called spinach, all belonging to different genera; there is the annual (summer and winter) spinach, New Zealand spinach which is also an annual, and the range named sea kale or spinach beet, or perpetual spinach which is biennial. There are several varieties of perpetual spinach which are of highly decorative value and with fleshy ribs of pink or red; all are good as spinach, as are the leaves of the white beetroot – see Beetroot.

SOIL

Well-dug and drained and manured, New Zealand doing best on lighter soils, perpetual on drier soils.

SOW

Annual spinach: March to September, $\frac{1}{2}$ to 1 inch deep in rows about 1 foot apart.
New Zealand spinach: late April to May, soaking seeds overnight first, 1 inch deep and in rows 3 feet apart.
Perpetual spinach: April to August, $\frac{1}{2}$ to 1 inch deep in rows about 15 inches apart.

Types of spinach: Annual, New Zealand and Seakale Beet

CULTIVATION

General – keep weeded and watered, especially in dry spells. Pests and diseases are generally of little importance but yellowing of leaves may indicate Spinach blight on annual spinach – affected leaves should be removed and burnt.

Annuals: thin to 9 inches if sown up to mid-July and 6 inches after as the plants are then less vigorous.

New Zealands: thin to 2 feet apart.

Perpetuals: thin to 15 inches apart.

CROP

When leaves are ready but do not strip plants or they will almost certainly die.

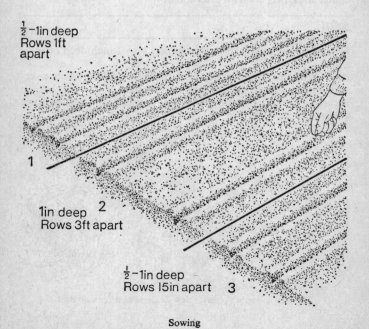

½–1in deep
Rows 1ft
apart

1

1in deep
Rows 3ft apart

2

½–1in deep
Rows 15in apart

3

Sowing

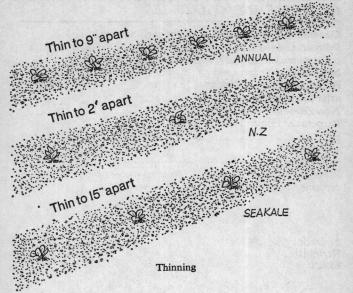

Thin to 9" apart   *ANNUAL*

Thin to 2' apart   *N.Z*

Thin to 15" apart   *SEAKALE*

Thinning

Cropping

RECOMMENDED VARIETIES

Annual – Longstanding Round, for early sowing.
   Broad Leaved Prickly, for late sowing.
   Greenmarket, for early and late sowing.
New Zealand – early sown.
Perpetual – Perpetual.
   Rhubarb Chard.
   Sea Kale or Silver Beet.

SWEDE

GENERAL

A winter vegetable which stores well making it the choice, where space is limited, rather than turnip – unless you definitely prefer the latter, of course. There are two main types – purple topped and bronze topped. Of these, the bronze topped, though slower growing than the purple, keeps best but in areas where club-root, which affects swedes, is prevalent then it is better to grow the purple topped 'Chignecto' which is particularly resistant to the fungus. Badly-drained and acid soils encourage infection so remedy these conditions if you have them by improving the soil – digging, adding materials to ensure good drainage and adding hydrated lime at about 14 lbs to 30 square yards should help you to grow swedes successfully.

SOIL

Well-drained, fertile soil, which is not acid, and has been improved by manure or compost for a previous crop, is best. Add a good all round fertiliser before sowing.

SOW

Unlike most vegetables, swede should be sown later in the south in order to reduce mildew infection. Sow early to mid-May in the north, late May to June in the south, in rows 18 inches apart, about ¾ to 1 inch deep.

CULTIVATION

Keep reasonably weed-free and moist while growing. Thin seedlings out to 9 to 12 inches apart. The main infections are club-root, mentioned under General above, and mildew, mentioned under Sow above. Pests are rarely troublesome.

CROP

From autumn to spring. Over winter in frosty weather, it is a good idea to lift some roots and store them.

RECOMMENDED VARIETIES

Purple Top.
Chignecto.*
Bronze Top.

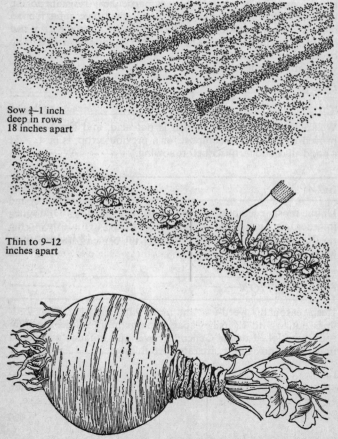

Sow ¾–1 inch
deep in rows
18 inches apart

Thin to 9–12
inches apart

A mature plant ready for the kitchen

SWEET CORN

GENERAL

Modern varieties of sweet corn have at last made this a possible vegetable for most gardeners, without creating too much trouble. Moreover, you do not need enormous beds for success. Fresh-cut sweet corn can be quite a revelation for flavour if you have not tasted it before. However, it is a luxury vegetable for a small garden if yield × area to grow is compared with other crops. From the top of the plant the male flower tassel drops its pollen, by wind or gravity, onto the female tassel which sprouts from a green, rather cigar-like sheath further down the stem. When fertilised, the sweet corn develops in this, taking a month or so to ripen.

SOIL

This is a crop that does not have to be grown on ground manured for a previous crop; dig in plenty of manure or compost, in the autumn. A warm, sunny spot should be chosen.

SOW

Indoors in April to plant out in May. Outdoors in May. Plant out or sow directly at $\frac{1}{2}$ inch deep, 15 to 18 inches apart in and between rows. Small squares of 5 plants can be grown among other plants in a bed or border; the 18 inch (or more) spacing should be used for the corner plants, the centre plant will then be just over 13 inches from all the others. One clear foot should be allowed all round the square.

CULTIVATION

Keep well-watered. Keep reasonably weed-free. Pests and diseases are not a bother.

CROP

Ripe cobs develop after fertilisation – the tassels turning brown, but check by lightly pressing a few seeds – they will burst if ripe.

Earliking F₁
John Innes F₁
Xtra Sweet F₁, Early Extra Sweet

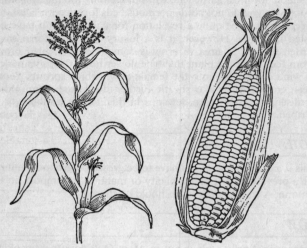

The head of a plant with the male tassels
at the top and young females below

A mature cob

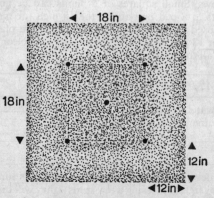

A way of growing sweet corn in the bed
or border of a small garden

TARRAGON

GENERAL

There are two varieties of tarragon: French tarragon is *Artemesia dracunculus* var. *sativa* and Russian, *A. d.* var. *inodora*. French tarragon is very superior in flavour but not always easy to obtain. Seed merely called 'Tarragon' is most likely to be of the inferior 'Russian' species. Indeed the seed of French tarragon is rarely fertile but plants, from cuttings or divisions are obtainable. French tarragon is useful in many sauces, for flavouring vinegar (wine vinegar naturally), in herb mixtures such as *fines herbes* for omelettes and for poultry and fish dishes. It is suitable for quick freezing and may also be preserved by sterilising in sealed glass jars – do not add anything to the leaves. The flavour is not so good if the leaves are dried. French tarragon is a shrub growing up to 2 to 3 feet in height and may be planted in a suitable garden border.

SOIL

Very well-drained and light soil, in a sunny spot.

SOW

Late autumn or spring – only 1 or 2 plants will be needed by most households. As they need replacing every three or four years due to a fall off in flavour, it is as well to have two growing which have been planted in different years replacing one at a time and so always having one ready for use.

CULTIVATION

Keep weed-free, and if the weather is very dry, watered, until established. Generally free of pest and disease troubles.

CROP

As required. For storage see General above.

RECOMMENDED VARIETIES

French tarragon

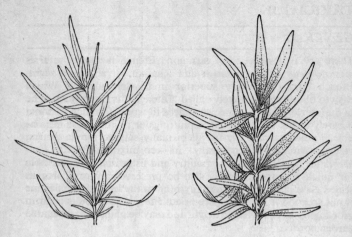

Types of tarragon: French and Russian

Plant tarragon in a prepared site

Tarragon may be kept by
sterilising in sealed glass jars,

THYME

GENERAL

There are few dishes in which thyme may not be used. Useful as a flavouring for soups, meat dishes, poultry, game and vegetables, the various thymes are also easy plants to grow. Which thymes you do grow, however, should depend on your own taste and probably upon which thymes are readily available. Most make attractive creeping or ground cover plants and may be grown between crazy paving stones. They are evergreen shrubs, generally available as rooted plants – cuttings or divisions – although seed of Garden thyme is also obtainable. The varieties often have descriptive names indicating the additional aromas they suggest, such as Lemon thyme and Caraway thyme. Some thymes also have decorative foliage, as does the golden-leaved form of Garden thyme, and the golden-leaved and silver variegated leaved forms of Lemon thyme.

SOIL

Well-drained and in a sunny position is best; does well in dry, limy conditions.

SOW

Spring.

CULTIVATION

Keep weed-free until established when its creeping and dense habit will start smothering weeds. Plants may get straggly and if trimming does not help with your variety, take cuttings with a heel, in late spring to early summer, to replace your older plants. Cuttings should be about 3 inches long and inserted either where you want them to grow, or in pots of suitable compost, such as John Innes seed or potting compost No. 1, and kept moist until growing away. Should you have difficulty in propagating out of doors, cuttings may also be grown on a window-sill – not sunny until established – and planted out the following spring to autumn. Pests and diseases are rarely a trouble.

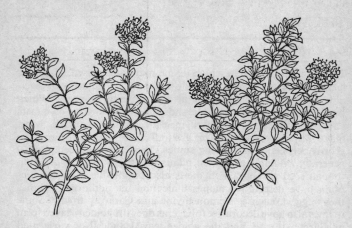

Some types of thyme: Wild and Garden

Thymes make good border plants

CROP

As required. Thyme may also be dried or quick frozen.

RECOMMENDED VARIETIES

Garden thyme, *Thymus vulgaris*.
Lemon thyme, *T. x citriodorus*.
Caraway thyme, *T. herba–barona*.
Larger wild thyme, *T. pulegioides*.

TOMATO

GENERAL

The development of the outdoor bush tomato brings this plant into the 'no bother to grow' class of plant. No doubt there will be many who keep to the old method of staking and training a single stem, pinching out and stopping as its culture requires. The advantages of the bush tomato are considerable for a small garden which cannot be frequently attended. Once the seedlings are planted out, apart from watering and the occasional feed, they should need no attention: leave them to branch, flower and set fruit. Two such plants may provide for a family of two or three but a heavy ripening of tomatoes does depend a great deal on the weather and if you have room plant three or four – they take up about 2 to 3 feet of space and grow up to 2 to $3\frac{1}{2}$ feet high, making ideal half-tub plants. You will need two to three times as many plants grown on a single stem to get equivalent crops. The choice is yours as to which type and which colour, for there are yellow varieties, which are considered by some to have a finer flavour then the red, and the striped yellow and red 'Tigerella'.

SOIL

Improve the soil by digging in manure or compost during the winter, early if the soil is heavy and late if light. A sunny sheltered position is best. Specially prepared bags of compost in which to grow tomatoes are available, and, while they save bother, are not exactly inexpensive. If growing in a tub, make sure that drainage is good and the soil enriched with manure or compost.

SOW

Under glass in March to April. Cover the seed box or pan with polythene or glass until the seedlings appear, when the cover should be removed. Make sure the seedlings get as much light as possible. Ideally the seedlings should be potted on into $3\frac{1}{2}$ inch pots when the first leaves have opened but I know many successful growers who, by limiting the number of seedlings per box, grow the plants on in the box until they are planted out.

Plant the seedlings out in May to June, keeping them well-watered. Bush tomatoes will then require little attention except to feed with a tomato fertiliser according to the instructions on the pack or bottle, and to have straw placed under the plant for the fruit to rest on and so be kept clean of soil and clear of slugs. Tomatoes to be grown on a single stem should be staked early, with 4 foot of the stake above ground, and all side shoots should be removed which appear in the leaf axils – do not pinch out the flower trusses which appear on the main stem. Stop further growth by pinching out the top shoot in early August. This measure helps swell and ripen the set fruits. When planting out, water in but then be sparing until the plants are established – if the weather is hot or dry they will need more – and then keep them well-watered. Feed with a tomato fertiliser according to the instructions given on the pack or bottle. Keep tied to the stakes as the plants grow. The main pests – which may not affect you – are the caterpillars of a moth which should be picked off and dealt with, and the potato eelworm which attacks the roots causing wilting, yellowing of leaves and stunts growth – deal with if the plant is badly affected by uprooting and burning. There is no remedy for this eelworm but neither tomatoes nor potatoes should be grown on infected soil again for a number of years.

Bush tomatoes may easily be grown in tubs

As the fruit ripens. Late in the season green tomatoes can often be ripened indoors; many achieve success by placing the unripened fruit in drawers while others favour hanging whole trusses up inside in front of a window. These green tomatoes may, of course, be used as they are for green tomato chutney, an excellent specific for tired meat.

Sowing the seed in boxes
kept on the window sill

Transplanted single stem tomatoes,
15–24 inches apart in rows 2½ feet apart

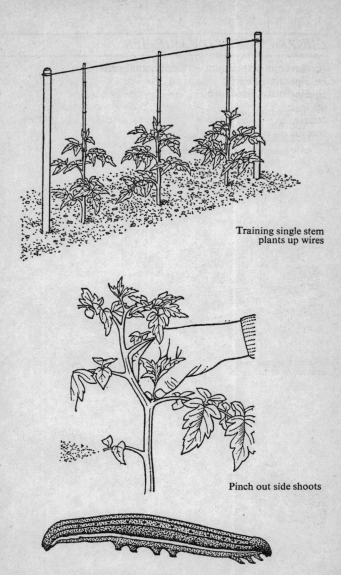

Training single stem
plants up wires

Pinch out side shoots

Caterpillars may be troublesome

Bush tomatoes – Roma – a Continental variety
    Sigmabush F_1.†
    Sleaford Abundance F_1.

Staking tomatoes:
    Alicante.
    Golden Sunrise† – yellow fruited.
    Marmande – a Continental variety.
    Moneymaker.

TURNIP

GENERAL

The various varieties of turnip make this an almost all the year round root crop and during the winter the leaves can provide 'greens'. The Milan varieties are early, the Jersey Navet (*navet* is the French name for turnip) may be sown from April through to July, Golden Ball is an excellent keeper which, sown late, may be used for winter greens, as may Early Green Top.

SOIL

Well-dug and deeply manured or composted, preferably on the light side and also in a sunny spot. Phosphate in the form of Superphosphate may be added before sowing.

SOW

From mid to late March for early crops; April to May for summer crops and July to late August for autumn and winter crops. Sow about $\frac{1}{2}$ inch deep in rows 1 foot or more apart. For leaf crops, sow in the autumn.

CULTIVATION

Thin the seedlings to 9 inches apart for early and summer crops and to 1 foot apart for later ones. Roots will be smaller if less space is allowed. Leaf crops will not need thinning. Keep moist and reasonably weed-free. Pests are usually not much trouble though flea beetles may eat holes in the leaves. Diseases are also usually not much trouble except for club-root in some areas and where it is prevalent liming the soil and improving the drainage will help. Calomel dusted in the rows before sowing will also help to control the fungus.

CROP

As required; winter turnips may be kept in the soil or stored, after lifting and cutting off the foliage in November.

Sow ½ inch deep
in rows 12 inches
apart

Thin to 9–12 inches apart

Some types of
turnip: Green
Top and Golden
Ball

RECOMMENDED VARIETIES

Red Purple (Milan) Top.
Milan White.
Manchester Market.
Golden Ball.
Marteau (Jersey Navet).